T0114297

JANE JACOBS

Dark Age Ahead

Jane Jacobs is the legendary author of *The Death and Life of Great American Cities,* a work that has never gone out of print and that has transformed the disciplines of urban planning and city architecture. Her other major works include *The Economy of Cities*, *Systems of Survival*, and *The Nature of Economies.* She died in 2006.

Dark
Age
Ahead

Dark
Age
Ahead

JANE JACOBS

VINTAGE BOOKS

A DIVISION OF RANDOM HOUSE, INC.

NEW YORK

FIRST VINTAGE BOOKS EDITION, MAY 2005

The Library of Congress has cataloged the Random House edition as follows:
Jacobs, Jane.
Dark age ahead / Jane Jacobs
p. cm.
Includes index.
1. Regression (Civilization). 2. Civilization—Philosophy.
I. Title.
CB19.J33   2004   901—dc22   2003066680

Vintage ISBN: 978-1-4000-7670-3

www.vintagebooks.com

146122990

To

SID ADILMAN AND

MARTHA SHUTTLEWORTH,

MERRY LEADING-EDGE EXPLORERS

CONTENTS

Dark
Age
Ahead

CHAPTER ONE

The Hazard

This is both a gloomy and a hopeful book.

The subject itself is gloomy. A Dark Age is a culture's dead end. We in North America and Western Europe, enjoying the many benefits of the culture conventionally known as the West, customarily think of a Dark Age as happening once, long ago, following the collapse of the Western Roman Empire. But in North America we live in a graveyard of lost aboriginal cultures, many of which were decisively finished off by mass amnesia in which even the memory of what was lost was also lost. Throughout the world Dark Ages have scrawled finis to successions of cultures receding far into the past. Whatever happened to the culture whose people produced the splendid Lascaux cave paintings some seventeen thousand years ago, in what is now southwestern France? Or the culture of the builders of ambitious stone and wood henges in Western Europe before the Celts arrived with their Iron Age technology and intricately knotted art?

Mass amnesia, striking as it is and seemingly weird, is the least mysterious of Dark Age phenomena. We all understand the harsh principle *Use it or lose it.* A failing or conquered culture can spiral down into a long decline, as has happened in most empires after their relatively short heydays of astonishing success. But in extreme cases, failing or conquered cultures can be genuinely lost, never to emerge again as living ways of being. The salient mystery of Dark Ages sets the stage for mass amnesia. People living in vigorous cultures typically treasure those cultures and resist any threat to them. How and why can a people so totally discard a formerly vital culture that it becomes literally lost?

This is a question that has practical importance for us here in North America, and possibly in Western Europe as well. Dark Ages are instructive, precisely because they are extreme examples of cultural collapse and thus more clear-cut and vivid than gradual decay. The purpose of this book is to help our culture avoid sliding into a dead end, by understanding how such a tragedy comes about, and thereby what can be done to ward it off and thus retain and further develop our living, functioning culture, which contains so much of value, so hard won by our forebears. We need this awareness because, as I plan to explain, we show signs of rushing headlong into a Dark Age.

Surely, the threat of losing all we have achieved, everything that makes us the vigorous society we are, cannot apply to us! How could it possibly happen to us? We have books, magnificent storehouses of knowledge about our culture; we have pictures, both still and moving, and oceans of other cultural information that every day wash through the Internet, the daily press, scholarly journals, the careful catalogs of museum exhibitions, the reports compiled by government bureaucracies on every subject from judicial decisions to regulations for earthquake-resistant buildings, and, of course, time capsules.

Dark Ages, surely, are pre-printing and pre–World Wide Web phenomena. Even the Roman classical world was skimpily documented in comparison with our times. With all our information, how could our culture be lost? Or even almost lost? Don't we have it as well preserved as last season's peach crop, ready to nourish our descendants if need be?

Writing, printing, and the Internet give a false sense of security about the permanence of culture. Most of the million details of a complex, living culture are transmitted neither in writing nor pictorially. Instead, cultures live through word of mouth and example. That is why we have cooking classes and cooking demonstrations, as well as cookbooks. That is why we have apprenticeships, internships, student tours, and on-the-job training as well as manuals and textbooks. Every culture takes pains to educate its young so that they, in their turn, can practice and transmit it completely. Educators and mentors, whether they are parents, elders, or schoolmasters, use books and videos if they have them, but they also speak, and when they are most effective, as teachers, parents, or mentors, they also serve as examples.

As recipients of culture, as well as its producers, people attend to countless nuances that are assimilated only through experience. Men, women, and children in Holland conduct themselves differently from men, women, and children in England, even though both share the culture of the West, and very differently from their counterparts in Turkey, Saudi Arabia, or Singapore. Travel writers, novelists, visual artists, and photographers draw attention to subtle, everyday differences in conduct rooted in experience, including the experience of differing cultural histories, but their glosses are unavoidably sketchy, compared with the experience of living a culture, soaking it up by example and word of mouth.

Another thing: a living culture is forever changing, without losing itself as a framework and context of change. The reconstruction of a culture is not the same as its restoration. In the fifteenth century, scholars and antiquarians set about reconstructing the lost classical culture of Greece and Rome from that culture's writing and artifacts. Their work was useful and remains so to this day; Western Europeans relearned their cultural derivations from it. But Europeans also plunged, beginning in the fifteenth century, into the post-Renaissance crises of the Enlightenment. Profoundly disturbing new knowledge entered a fundamentalist and feudal framework so unprepared to receive it that some scientists were excommunicated and their findings rejected by an establishment that had managed to accept reconstructed classicism—and used it to refute newer knowledge. Copernicus's stunning proofs forced educated people to realize that the earth is not the center of the universe, as reconstructed classical culture would have it. This and other discoveries, especially in the basic sciences of chemistry and physics, pitted the creative culture of the Enlightenment against the reconstructed culture of the Renaissance, which soon stood, ironically, as a barrier to cultural development of the West—a barrier formed by canned and preserved knowledge of kinds which we erroneously may imagine can save us from future decline or forgetfulness.

Dark Ages are horrible ordeals, incomparably worse than the temporary amnesia sometimes experienced by stunned survivors of earthquakes, battles, or bombing firestorms who abandon customary routines while they search for other survivors, grieve, and grapple with their own urgent needs, and who may forget the horrors they have witnessed, or try to. But later on, life for survivors continues for the most part as before, after having been suspended for the emergency.

During a Dark Age, the mass amnesia of survivors becomes permanent and profound. The previous way of life slides into an abyss of forgetfulness, almost as decisively as if it had not existed. Henri Pirenne, a great twentieth-century Belgian economic and social historian, says that the famous Dark Age which followed the collapse of the Western Roman Empire reached its nadir some six centuries later, about 1000 C.E. Here, sketched by two French historians, is the predicament of French peasantry in that year:

> The peasants . . . are half starved. The effects of chronic malnourishment are conspicuous in the skeletons exhumed. . . . The chafing of the teeth . . . indicates a grass-eating people, rickets, and an overwhelming preponderance of people who died young. . . . Even for the minority that survived infancy, the average life span did not exceed the age of forty. . . . Periodically the lack of food grows worse. For a year or two there will be a great famine; the chroniclers described the graphic and horrible episodes of this catastrophe, complacently and rather excessively conjuring up people who eat dirt and sell human skin. . . . There is little or no metal; iron is reserved for weapons.

So much had been forgotten in the forgetful centuries: the Romans' use of legumes in crop rotation to restore the soil;

how to mine and smelt iron and make and transport picks for miners, and hammers and anvils for smiths; how to harvest honey from hollow-tile hives doubling as garden fences. In districts where even slaves had been well clothed, most people wore filthy rags.

Some three centuries after the Roman collapse, bubonic plague, hitherto unknown in Europe, crept in from North Africa, where it was endemic, and exploded into the first of many European bubonic plague epidemics. The Four Horsemen of the Apocalypse, conventionally depicted as Famine, War, Pestilence, and Death, had already been joined by a fifth demonic horseman, Forgetfulness.

A Dark Age is not merely a collection of subtractions. It is not a blank; much is added to fill the vacuum. But the additions break from the past and themselves reinforce a loss of the past. In Europe, languages that derived from formerly widely understood Latin diverged and became mutually incomprehensible. Everyday customs, rituals, and decorations diverged as old ones were lost; ethnic awarenesses came to the fore, often antagonistically; the embryos of nation-states were forming.

Citizenship gave way to serfdom; old Roman cities and towns were largely deserted and their underpopulated remnants sank into poverty and squalor; their former amenities, such as public baths and theatrical performances, became not even a memory. Gladiatorial battles and hungry wild animals unleashed upon prisoners were forgotten, too, but here and there, in backwaters, the memory of combat between a man on foot and a bull was retained because it was practiced. Diets changed, with gruel displacing bread, and salt fish and wild fowl almost displacing domesticated meat. Rules of inheritance and property holding changed. The composition of households changed drastically with conversion of Rome's traditional family-sized farms to feudal estates. Methods of warfare and ostensible reasons for warfare changed as the state and its laws gave way to exactions and oppressions by warlords.

Writers disappeared, along with readers and literacy, as schooling became rare. Religion changed as Christianity, formerly an obscure cult among hundreds of obscure cults, won enough adherents to become dominant and to be accepted as the state religion by Constantine, emperor of the still intact Eastern Roman Empire, and then, also as the state religion, in territorial remnants of the vanished Western Empire. The very definitions of virtue and the meaning of life changed. In Western Christendom, sexuality became highly suspect.

In sum, during the time of mass amnesia, not only was most classical culture forgotten, and what remained coarsened; but also, Western Europe underwent the most radical and thoroughgoing revolution in its recorded history—a political, economic, social, and ideological revolution that was unexamined and even largely unnoticed, as such, while it was under way. In the last desperate years before Western Rome's collapse, local governments had been expunged by imperial decree and were replaced by a centralized military despotism, not a workable organ for governmental judgments and reflections.

Similar phenomena are to be found in the obscure Dark Ages that bring defeated aboriginal cultures to a close. Many subtractions combine to erase a previous way of life, and everything changes as a richer past converts to a meager present and an alien future. During the conquest of North America by Europeans, an estimated twenty million aboriginals succumbed to imported diseases, warfare, and displacement from lands on which they and their hundreds of different cultures depended.

Their first response to the jolts of European invasion was to try to adapt familiar ways of life to the strange new circumstances. Some groups that had been accustomed to trading with one another, for example, forged seemingly workable trade links with the invaders. But after more conquerors crowded in, remnants of aboriginal survivors were herded into isolated reservations. Adaptations of the old cultures became impossible and thus no longer relevant; so, piece by piece, the old cultures were shed. Some pieces were relinquished voluntarily in emulation of the conquerors, or surrendered for the sake of the invaders' alcohol, guns, and flour; most slipped away from disuse and forgetfulness.

As in Europe after Rome's collapse, everything changed for aboriginal survivors during the forgetful years: education of children; religions and rituals; the composition of households and societies; food; clothing; habitations; recreations; laws and recognized systems of ownership and land use; concepts of justice, dignity, shame, esteem. Languages changed, with many becoming extinct; crafts, skills—everything was gone. In sum, the lives of aboriginals had been revolutionized, mostly by outside forces but also, to a very minor extent, from within.

In the late twentieth century, as some survivors gradually became conscious of how much had been lost, they began behaving much like the scholarly pioneers of the fifteenth-century Italian Renaissance who searched for relics of classical Greek and Roman culture. Cree and Cherokee, Navajo and Haida groped for fragments of lost information by searching out old records and artifacts dispersed in their conquerors' museums and private collections. Jeered at by an uncomprehending white public of cultural winners, they began impolitely demanding the return of ancestral articles of clothing and decoration, of musical instruments, of masks, even of the bones of their dead, in attempts to retrieve what their peoples and cultures had been like before their lives were transformed by mass amnesia and unsought revolution.

When the abyss of lost memory by a people becomes too deep and too old, attempts to plumb it are futile. The Ainu, Caucasian aborigines of Japan, have a known modern history similar in some ways to that of North American aboriginals. Centuries before the European invasion of North America, the Ainu lost their foraging territories to invading ancestors of the modern Japanese. Surviving remnants of Ainu were settled in isolated reservations, most on Hokkaido, Japan's northernmost island, where they still live. The Ainu remain a mysterious people, to themselves as well as to others. Physical characteristics proclaim their European ancestry; they may be related to Norse peoples. But where in Europe they came from can only be conjectured. They retain no information about their locations or cultures there, nor by what route they reached Japan, nor why they traveled there. (See note, p. 179.)

Cultures that triumphed in unequal contests between conquering invaders and their victims have been meticulously analyzed by a brilliant twenty-first-century historian and scientist, Jared Diamond, who has explained his analyses in a splendidly accessible book, *Guns, Germs, and Steel.* He writes that he began his exploration with a question put to him by a youth in New Guinea, asking why Europeans and Americans were successful and rich. The advantages that Diamond explored and the patterns he traces illuminate all instances of cultural wipeout.

Diamond argues persuasively that the difference between conquering and victim cultures is not owing to genetic discrepancies in intelligence or other inborn personal abilities among peoples, as racists persist in believing. He holds that, apart from variations in resistance to various diseases, the fates of cultures are not genetically influenced, let alone determined. But, he writes, successful invaders and conquerors have historically possessed certain crucial advantages conferred on them long ago by the luck of what he calls biogeography. The cultural ancestors of winners, he says, got head starts as outstandingly productive farmers and herders, producing ample and varied foods that could support large and dense populations.

Large and dense populations—in a word, cities—were able to support individuals and institutions engaged in activities other than direct food production. For example, such societies could support specialists in tool manufacturing, pottery making, boatbuilding, and barter, could organize and enforce legal codes, and could create priesthoods for celebrating and spreading religions, specialists for keeping accounts, and armed forces for defense and aggression.

Diamond's identifications of basic causes of discrepancies in power among cultures boil down to good or bad geographical luck. His resulting causes boil down to size and density of populations and consequent differences in technological and organizational specialization. All these factors can be quantified.

This analysis worked so well for explaining the historical outcomes of conflicts that ranged over all the continents, and also on islands extending from the Arctic to the South Pacific, that Diamond hoped he had created the foundation for a genuine science of human history—a true, hard science, based on facts as solid and measurable as those underlying physics or chemistry, and as reliable for predicting future outcomes of conflict. It seemed to him that only a couple of loose ends needed tying.

One such was how cultures lost their memories. This was not hard for Diamond to explain as a consequence of *Use it or lose it.* He took as a vivid example the Tasmanians, who were nearly exterminated by invading Europeans in the nineteenth century. They were the most technologically primitive people to be recorded in modern history. They had no way of making fire, no boomerangs or spear throwers, no specialized stone tools, no canoes, no sewing needles, no ways of catching fish. Yet their parent culture, on the Australian mainland, had all these technologies. Presumably the Tasmanians did too, some ten thousand years previously, when they populated their island by traveling from the mainland over a prehistoric land bridge. Diamond remarks that a culture can lose a given technology for many reasons. Perhaps a certain raw material is in short supply; perhaps all the skilled artisans in a generation meet with tragedy. Whenever the Tasmanians lost an element of their culture, the loss would have been temporary had they still been in communication with the mainland, but because they were not, each loss became permanent.

The second loose end, however, threatened to unravel Diamond's whole fabric, as he recognized. According to his analyses, China and Mesopotamia, both of which had early and long leads over European cultures, should have securely maintained those leads, but did not. While neither experienced the extreme of a Dark Age, both succumbed to long declines, insidiously growing poverty, and backwardness relative to Europe. They inform us, as do the unedifying terminations of all great empires in the past, that strong and successful cultures can fail. The difference between these failures and those of conquered aboriginal cultures is that the death or the stagnated moribundity of formerly unassailable and vigorous cultures is caused not by assault from outside but by assault from within, that is, by internal rot in the form of fatal cultural turnings, not recognized as wrong turnings while they occur or soon enough afterward to be correctable. Time during which corrections can be made runs out because of mass forgetfulness.

Mesopotamia, the so-called Fertile Crescent of the Tigris and Euphrates rivers—traditionally thought to be the site of the biblical Garden of Eden—in historical times has centered on the fabled city of Baghdad. For some nine thousand years, starting in about 8500 B.C.E., almost every major innovation adopted in ancient Europe had originated in or very near the Fertile Crescent: grain cultivation; writing; brickmaking, masonry engineering, and construction; the wheel; weaving; pottery making; irrigation. Just as Diamond's attempted science of human history would predict, the Fertile Crescent was the seat of the ancient world's earliest empires: Sumer, Babylon, Assyria.

Yet with all its seemingly unbeatable advantages, something went so wrong in the Fertile Crescent that, as Diamond says, it is now absurd to couple "Fertile Crescent" with "world leader in food production. Today's ephemeral wealth[,] . . . based on the single non-renewable resource of oil, conceals the region's long-standing fundamental poverty and difficulty feeding itself."

Diamond asked himself how so gifted a region could lose its early, long lead over Europe. By 115 C.E., Mesopotamia had been conquered by Rome and became a Roman province. This was no temporary setback. Over the course of the next eighteen centuries, the region was passed around from invader to invader, eventually falling into the hands of the British Empire and Western oil corporations; a new chapter, of conflicts over oil, is not yet finished.

Diamond says the lead was lost through environmental ignorance. In ancient times, much of the Fertile Crescent and eastern Mediterranean was covered with forests. But to obtain more farmland and more timber, and to satisfy the plaster industry's relentless demands for wood fuel, the forests were cut faster than they could regenerate. Denuded valleys silted up, and intensified irrigation led to salt accumulations in the soil. Overgrazing by goats, allowing new growth no start in life, sealed the destruction. The damage had become irreversible, Diamond says, by 400 B.C.E. What escaped earlier has been done in recently: "The last forests . . . in modern Jordan . . . were felled by Ottoman Turks during railroad construction just before World War I." Most of the last wetlands, the great reed marshes of southern Iraq, with their complex ecology of plants, mammals, insects, birds, and human beings, too—the "Marsh Arabs" who had occupied these lands for some five thousand years—fell to a drainage scheme undertaken for political reasons by Saddam Hussein in the 1990s, creating another barren, salt-encrusted desert.

Northern and Western Europe pulled abreast of Mesopotamia, then surpassed it, says Diamond, "not because [Europeans] have been wiser but because they had the good luck to live in a more robust environment with higher rainfall, in which vegetation grows quickly." Also, they herded cows and sheep, not goats.

The Fertile Crescent, along with the rest of the Middle East, reasserted its creative lead—not in food production but in science—during the triumphs of the Islamic empires. Islam was the most successful political, military, religious, and cultural entity of its time, asserting dominance from the eighth to the fifteenth centuries, westward through North Africa and Spain, eastward to South Asia. So far ahead of Europe was the scientific knowledge of Islam that most scientific and literary works from the classical period which Renaissance scholars finally obtained had been translated from Greek and Latin into Arabic; Islamic scholars later retranslated these texts into Latin for scholars in European Christendom. During this period, our ancestral European culture also obtained from Islam the nimble signs that we still call Arabic numerals, and that are indispensable to our mathematics and all the achievements of measuring and reasoning that mathematics has made possible. Arabic numerals originated in the Fertile Crescent and India; the source of their most original and portentous addition, the zero, was the Fertile Crescent. The first known European mathematical use of the zero was in a Spanish manuscript dated 976 C.E. and believed to be derived from a Latin translation of a Baghdad work.

Although Diamond does not go into the second cultural deadening of the Fertile Crescent that brought to an end the second burst of world-altering scientific creativity there, another scholar, Karen Armstrong, has identified the point of no return as 1492, the year Ferdinand and Isabella drove the Muslims from Spain—their last important European foothold—in determination to expunge from their realm Muslims, Jews,

Christian heretics, and other infidels. From then until the start of the nineteenth century, Mesopotamia deliberately attempted to shield itself from influences coming from the outside world.

Cultural xenophobia is a frequent sequel to a society's decline from cultural vigor. Someone has aptly called self-imposed isolation a fortress mentality. Armstrong describes it as a shift from faith in *logos,* reason, with its future-oriented spirit, "always . . . seeking to know more and to extend . . . areas of competence and control of the environment," to *mythos,* meaning conservatism that looks backward to fundamentalist beliefs for guidance and a worldview.

A fortress or fundamentalist mentality not only shuts itself off from dynamic influences originating outside but also, as a side effect, ceases influencing the outside world. Fortunately for our own culture, before Mesopotamia succeeded in entirely sealing itself off, some of its talented and open-minded scientists fled to northern Italy, where they joined Galileo, Vesalius, and other precursors of the Enlightenment, who had their own hard battles to fight against spiritual and intellectual fundamentalism. Mesopotamian scientists helped make the University of Padua a preeminent world center of reason when our own ancestral culture needed rescue from the stultifying ideas that all valuable thought had already been thought and that disturbing new ideas—for example, that the earth is eons older than *mythos* admits—are unnecessary or dangerous.

China had much the same original advantages as the Fertile Crescent, plus greater rainfall, and retained its early lead longer. The large and dense population of medieval China enabled it to become the world leader in technology. Among its many innovations were cast iron, the compass, gunpowder, paper, printing with movable type, windmills, navigation equipment of all kinds, paper money, porcelain, and unparalleled silk spinning, weaving, and dyeing. China ruled the seas in the early fifteenth century. It sent vast numbers of cargo ships, called treasure fleets, across the Indian Ocean to the east coast of Africa, decades before Columbus crossed the Atlantic. The treasure fleets consisted of hundreds of ships, each as much as four hundred feet long. A fleet was manned by as many as twenty-eight thousand sailors. Centuries before the British Royal Navy learned to combat scurvy with rations of lime juice on long sea voyages, the Chinese had solved that problem by supplying ships with ordinary dried beans, which were moistened as needed to make bean sprouts, a rich source of vitamin C.

Diamond asked himself why Chinese ships didn't colonize Europe before Vasco da Gama's three little Portuguese ships launched Europe's colonization of East Asia. "Why didn't Chinese ships . . . colonize America's west coast? Why did China lose its technological lead to formerly so backward Europe?"

In this case, the turning point was almost whimsical, like the plot of a musical or an operetta. In the early fifteenth century, a political power struggle was waged between two factions in the Chinese imperial bureaucracy. The losing faction had championed treasure fleets and taken an interest in their leadership and well-being. The winning faction asserted its success by abruptly calling a halt to voyages, forbidding further ocean voyaging, and dismantling shipyards.

In the complex Chinese culture, the loss of the great shipyards must have reverberated through the economy, affecting many other activities; so did the loss of the far-flung import and export trade. In 1433, with a capricious policy emerging from a tempest in a teapot, China's long stagnation began. A deeper cause than the court intrigue, Diamond points out, was that China was so tightly unified politically that "one decision stopped fleets over the whole of China." He contrasts this with Columbus's potential opportunities for sponsorship. After Columbus was turned down by the Duke of Anjou, and then in succession by the King of Portugal, the Duke of Medina-Sedona, and the Count of Meda-Celi, he finally hit the jackpot with Isabella and Ferdinand of Spain. Europe's political fragmentation and its therefore decentralized decision making afforded crucial opportunities to Columbus and other explorers that were denied to mariners of the richer and more advanced Chinese. Unity, like many good things, is good only in moderation. The same can be said of disunity. In 1477, when a Chinese attempt was made to revive intercontinental ocean trading, the vice president of the War Ministry not only forbade it but destroyed all the documents regarding previous trading voyages. He called them "deceitful exaggerations of bizarre things, far removed from the testimony of people's eyes and ears," and said the ships had brought home nothing but "betel, bamboo staves, grape wine, pomegranates, ostrich eggs and such like odd things." Loss of charts and records from the archives ended medieval China's interest in the outside world, as well as the period of exploration.

China's wrong turning, capricious though it was, carried the double blow of surrender of its technological lead and simultaneous retreat into a fortress mentality. In China's case, the *mythos* for which *logos* was surrendered was Confucianism, an intellectual and social bequest from a sage of the long-distant past which was believed to contain all necessary precepts for the conduct of human beings in their relationships with one another and with their environment.

Diamond's analysis of winners and losers, elegantly precise

and predictable wherever the forces at work were geography, climate, plants, animals, microorganisms, and demography, turned mushy and unreliable as soon as human decisions entered the equation. Yet, as he himself was the first to admit, a science of human history that omits the behavior of human beings is an absurdity. His brilliant analysis, as is, explains most outcomes of unequal contests between cultural winners and losers. But I think he limited its explanatory power unnecessarily by the way he posed his initial question: *What are the advantages that enable cultural conquerors to win conflicts with losers?*

Suppose we turn the question upside down and ask: *What dooms losers?* The answer to the new question, cast in the form of a principle, runs something like this: *Losers are confronted with such radical jolts in circumstances that their institutions cannot adapt adequately, become irrelevant, and are dropped.* This principle leaves scope for changes and jolts that arise within a culture, as well as changes and jolts imposed from outside.

A common example of a change imposed from the outside is the seizure by a conqueror of a hunting society's territory. As a consequence, both the practice and lore of successful hunting is lost from those cultures. The oldest resident of Fort Yukon, a man of about seventy in a predominantly American Indian community within the Arctic Circle, explained in 1994, "Our young fellows get me to tell them about the old hunting life. They think it would be so wonderful and exciting to follow it again instead of the dull jobs the school tries to prepare them for. But they don't realize how hard and chancy hunting was. They don't know enough to survive in the bush."

An example of a jolt from within is the overfishing of cod that has idled fishermen in Newfoundland villages. Some fishermen adapt by overfishing other groundfish and crabs, some by taking jobs in factories (almost always short-lived enterprises lured in and subsidized by the province); many, if they are young, emigrate to cities elsewhere in Canada; and others temporize and live on hopes that wealth from offshore oil drilling will trickle down to them in time. How to fish for cod is not forgotten yet, but it will be if the fish stocks don't recover soon, which they show no sign of doing after a decade-long moratorium.

Jolts from inside and outside are not basically different. What is lost from Diamond's erstwhile science of human history when we factor in human decisions is the aim he had of creating a genuinely hard science. Bringing in human decisions, as he did and as we must, changes the science itself, from a hard science to a soft one.

Some people think optimistically that if things get bad enough, they will get better because of the reaction of beneficent pendulums. When a culture is working wholesomely, beneficent pendulum swings—effective feedback—do occur. Corrective stabilization is one of the great services of democracy, with its feedback to rulers from the protesting and voting public. Stabilization is also one of the great services of some commercial innovations which, in concert with markets, shift production and consumption away from resources plagued by the high costs of diminishing returns, to substitutes or to other locales of production.

But powerful persons and groups that find it in their interest to prevent adaptive corrections have many ways of thwarting self-organizing stabilizers—through deliberately contrived subsidies and monopolies, for example. Or circumstances may have allowed cultural destruction to drift to a point where the jolts of correction appear more menacing than downward drift. Gibbon's *Decline and Fall of the Roman Empire* is stuffed with instances of drift that became monstrous and ultimately proved impossible to correct. For instance, as shortfalls in the Roman treasury—which had their own economic causes—made it impossible to pay Rome's legions adequately and on time, elite guard units took into their own hands the power of choosing emperors in hopes of ensuring their own well-being. This made a shambles of orderly government successions and policies, including budgets for supporting the legions—a shambles that with time grew worse, not better. In the half century from 235 C.E. to 284 C.E., Rome had twenty-six army-acclaimed emperors, who, with only one exception, succumbed to public assassinations or private murders. Rome's other major institutions, such as the Senate and the empire's diplomatic structures, were implicated in this bizarre sequence, either through their own corruption or by pernicious drifts of their own.

The human causes of Rome's collapse have been studied minutely, and one thing that can be learned is that everything is connected with everything else, not only in its consequences but also in its causes. We may be sure that the story of the desertification of the Fertile Crescent, cited by Diamond, was not simple. At the least, corrective adaptation that would have threatened the plaster industry (which was so voraciously consuming forests for fuel) and would have handicapped goatherding and its dependent industries must have appeared, at the time, to be less feasible than continuing to ruin the land itself.

In the case of China's self-imposed stagnation as a by-product of political squabbling, we must bring in the usual complicating fact that everything was connected to everything else, and add the reality I mentioned earlier: that even in a literate and archive-keeping society, which medieval China was, time for corrective action is finite: culture resides mainly in people's heads and in the examples people set, and is subject therefore to natural mortality. Thousands of details of shipbuilding, equipping, navigating, and trading practices obviously went into the complicated creation, finance, and operation of treasure fleets. As the people who had competently maintained this organizational wonder died off, so must have cultural competence to follow in their footsteps.

People get used to losses (fortunately, or life would be unbearable) and take absences for granted. So it must have been, eventually, with Chinese ocean voyages. In North America, a couple of decades ago, it was common to hear residents remark, as they locked up for a short departure from home, that they never used to need to lock their doors. Nowadays, the remark is seldom heard. People who once didn't need to lock their doors have gradually died off, and so even the memory of what has been lost is now almost lost. As for reconstituting that particular security, what with everything connecting to everything else—the illegal drug trade, police corruption, racism, poverty, and inadequate education—theft and robbery are so intractably complex as to defy solution. The only reason I know that unlocked-door security is actually possible (although my mother used to frequently comment about formerly not having to lock the door) is that I have experienced unlocked security, with amazement, during a visit to Tokyo, Kyoto, and Osaka in 1972.

The collapse of one sustaining cultural institution enfeebles others, making it more likely that others will give way. With each collapse, still further ruin becomes more likely, until finally the whole enfeebled, intractable contraption crashes. Beneficent corrections of deterioration are not guaranteed.

A culture is unsalvageable if stabilizing forces themselves become ruined and irrelevant. This is what I fear for our own culture, and why I have written this cautionary book in hopeful expectation that time remains for corrective actions. Each correction benefits others, making connections within the culture beneficial instead of malignant.

In the five chapters that follow, I single out five pillars of our culture that we depend on to stand firm, and discuss what seem to me ominous signs of their decay. They are in process of becoming irrelevant, and so are dangerously close to the brink of lost memory and cultural uselessness. These five jeopardized pillars are

- community and family (the two are so tightly connected they cannot be considered separately)
- higher education
- the effective practice of science and science-based technology (again, so tightly connected they cannot be considered separately)
- taxes and governmental powers directly in touch with needs and possibilities
- self-policing by the learned professions.

It may seem surprising that I do not single out such failings as racism, profligate environmental destruction, crime, voters' distrust of politicians and thus low turnouts for elections, and the enlarging gulf between rich and poor along with attrition of the middle class. Why not those five, rather than the five I have selected to concentrate upon? Surely the second five indicate serious cultural dysfunction. Perhaps my judgment is wrong, but I think these second five are symptoms of breakdown in the five I have chosen to discuss. Furthermore, many North Americans are already aware of them as dangerous flaws and are trying to focus on intelligent corrections.

The weaknesses I single out in the five pillars are less recognized, I think. These pillars are crucial to the culture and are insidiously decaying. Other institutions may be as deserving of alarmed attention. Hindsight may well expose my blind spots. Indeed, it surely will if we continue drifting, heedless of our culture's well-being. I can only apologize for being less omniscient than I should be as I take up a responsibility—which I hope readers will also assume—for trying to do the small bit I can to give stabilizing corrections a push. A culture is a vast and obdurate entity, difficult to divert from a mistaken course upon which it has set. Following my discussion of the decay of the five cultural pillars, I attempt practical suggestions for reversing some intractable deteriorations.

My last chapter returns to patterns of Dark Ages and less extreme deteriorations, and puts them into larger context than our own vexations. It also suggests why our predicament—the shift to postagrarianism—is so jolting that if our culture and our contemporaries' pull through more or less intact, we will all deserve posterity's gratitude.

Although the chapters that follow are structured as a collection of warnings, this book should not be mistaken for prophecy. Life is full of surprises—some of them good, with large, beneficial, totally unforeseen consequences. Prophecy is for people too ignorant of history to be aware of that, or for charlatans. However, by definition, we can't rely on surprise rescues; mostly we must lie in the beds we make on the mattresses our culture provides.

One aspect of luck is that companion cultures can be rescued by one another, in part by welcoming exiles and their ways. This has often happened. I have already given some examples of the remarkable aid given our ancestral culture centuries ago by the culture of Mesopotamia, of all places, when it was already deeply in trouble itself. In the following six chapters I have confined my analysis to North America because that is the culture I know best. However, its direct ancestral culture is that of Western Europe, which has many branches other than the North American offshoot. Among the disturbing phenomena I observe is that the same ills besetting the United States and Canada menace other branches of the West, if not yet as acutely. Maybe the most useful service of the cautions that follow is to alert societies that suppose they have an exemplary model in America; they would do well to pause, be wary, and sift carefully, discriminating between much that is constructive and vigorous, or at worst merely novel and harmless, and much that is destructive and deadening.

CHAPTER TWO

Families Rigged to Fail

You probably know them personally, but in any case you've seen them in a thousand advertisements: the father, the mother, the little boy, and his older sister, alighting from their new car at the charming small-town church; or smiling at home as the mother, equipped with a squirt bottle of detergent and a plastic sponge, whisks away the stains of spillages, everything restored shiny as new. Sometimes, for the approval of women customers, the father does the magic cleanup.

This is the nuclear family: a biological unit. With such minor modifications as a third generation rather than only two, or the inclusion of grown children—uncles and aunts— as collateral and probably temporary members, this unit stands, and has long stood, as the ur-unit of culture, whether rich, like the one in the paragraph above, or poor, like the family of a serf.

The nuclear family has traditionally been expected by its

own members and by others to fulfill, also, the functions of a household. The household, the other elementary microcosm of culture, is an economic unit. It provides its members, whoever they may be, with material necessities of life: food, clothing, shelter, and, if need be, transportation and detergents. The two units, one biological, the other economic, commonly overlap but are not necessarily the same.

We might, offhand, expect families to have been the more successful of the two at adapting to change—after all, biology is more basic than economy. But it has been usual for households to be more adaptable and resilient than families when subjected to stresses and jolts, while at the same time maintaining their elementary functions. This world contains households with enormous varieties of members: concubines; apprentices and other students; roomers and boarders; all manner of servants, from governesses and tutors to scullery maids and pages. Our modern culture still includes numerous households of types that proliferated wildly during the disorder of the Dark Age after Western Rome's collapse. Monasteries and convents are nonfamily, even antifamily households, constitutionally disconnected from the biological unit. A few huge feudal households remain in Europe, embracing both rich and poor biological families, but immensely more effective as economic than as biological units. Monasteries and, to a lesser extent, convents have been resourceful and varied in devising means for meeting household expenses. Their offshoot households have included boarding schools and orphanages. Offshoot households of parishes have been poorhouses, workhouses, and early hospitals. Most standing armies, from their beginning, have incorporated mess halls, uniforms, and barracks for nonofficer ranks. To venture a generalization: households, adaptable as they are, take over functions that families are at a loss to fill.

While politicians, clergy, creators of advertisements, and other worthies assert stoutly that the family is the foundation of society, the nuclear family, as an institution, is currently in grave trouble. Almost half of marriages—more in some places—end in divorce, in Canada after an average duration of 13.7 years, not long enough to rear children to adulthood.* Increasingly marriage is bypassed altogether or postponed into early middle age, a major reason, demographers say, for reduced birthrates.

Although high divorce rates cut across all income classes, as do drug abuse, juvenile delinquency, and spouse abuse, a brief discussion of family finances is the speediest way of acknowledging the frequent gap between what is expected of a family-household, and the means of fulfilling expectations.

For almost forty years, starting in the mid- and late 1930s, the median income of an American or Canadian family was sufficient to cover the mortgage costs of a median-priced house or the rent of a median-priced apartment. "Median" means, statistically, that half of whatever is being measured falls below the median, and half above. But at some point in the 1970s, the two figures—median shelter cost and median income—slipped seriously out of whack. The disconnection showed up clearly in the Canadian census of 1981. At about the same time, U.S. economic statistics showed that the purchase of a "median" house required an income that only 10

---

*A poorly conceived statistic. Common knowledge tells us that it must be compounded from a large number of very short marriages (two to five years long) and a smaller number of lasting marriages (upwards of twenty years long).

percent of families could claim. Ninety percent could no longer afford to buy a "median" house. It took only two people to produce children, but on average two by themselves could no longer afford to purchase or rent shelter for them.

The gap jolted renters, those who had not bought a house during the time when incomes and shelter costs corresponded more closely. In the years that followed, renters spent increasingly high proportions of their incomes on shelter, to the point that, for many, at least half their income was consumed by rent, leaving too little for everything else. A similar discrepancy showed up in England.

Homeless people who slept on the street or found minimal shelter in doorways, under bridges, or in shanties contrived of tarpaulins and cardboard tended to be single and were often afflicted with multiple health or other problems. The poor and disabled are always the first to alert us to social breakdowns. If their plight worsens or their numbers increase, it is prudent for cushioned members of a culture to take notice. In a Canadian magazine article published in 1984 and a book published the same year, I drew attention to an alarming gap between the cost of shelter and income. I received only one bit of economic feedback. It was from the director of a neoconservative economic think tank in Vancouver. He took exception to my statement that "a condition formerly normal only in poor parts of the United States had become normal for the nation." He replied to the editor of the magazine, as follows:

Now, the fact is that nearly all of the houses in the United States are occupied. Since only ten percent of the population can, apparently, afford housing, this implies that ninety percent of those who own housing in the United States cannot afford to do so. An obviously ridiculous situation. What Jacobs does not point out is that those rising house prices over the past several decades have also enhanced the wealth of home owners in the United States, most of whom are living in their most significant material asset. It is a simple arithmetic fact that the moment at which the median family in the United States cannot afford to purchase the median-priced house, the price of the median house will begin to fall. Provided, only, of course, that in calculating income we do not ignore the implicit income from most families' most important asset.

If this means anything, it must mean that the inflated wealth of those who already own houses cancels the plight of families priced out of the market. In one sense, something like that has happened from the viewpoint of the economy taken as a whole. In Toronto, home ownership rates have increased, rising to a record 61.5 percent of homes occupied by owners in 2002, compared with 54 percent in 2000, even though average house prices increased about 7 percent a year. The secret is low inflation rates (with the exception of house prices), which permit low mortgage and other borrowing rates. As prices of houses and condominiums rise, owners can continually borrow more against the rising value of these assets. In Canada, ratios of household debt to household income are thus at record high levels.

The miracle of money growing on houses operates even more potently in the United States, where mortgage interest is deductible from income tax and where purchases of resale houses reached record high levels in 2002, as their prices rose to record high levels and mortgage interest rates fell to record low levels. Perhaps the conservative think-tank economist quoted above foresaw and welcomed this bubble. It will burst, either if other rising prices significantly push up inflation rates, hence also interest rates, or else if house-price inflation slows, halts, or retreats. The critic is right that in this case median incomes and median house and condominium prices will once again coincide more closely.

This has not, however, canceled or even eased the plight of renters. Houses with ever higher prices do not trickle down to them. In the years since 1995, not only have the numbers of homeless in Toronto increased but also, as a new generation of poor young families has appeared, the homeless have come to include families who are crowded into a motel room or broken up so members can qualify for dormitory-type public shelters. Families on welfare and the "working poor," subsisting on low wages that often approximate welfare incomes, are of course worst off. They scrape by, when weekly income runs out sooner than the days of the week, by using charitable food banks and by borrowing either food or money from family and friends. Families of two in Toronto who use food banks spend an average of 67 percent of their income on rent; families of four, 70 percent. This typically left them, in early 2003, with only about $3.65 Canadian (about $2.40 U.S.) a day per person to cover food, clothing, transportation, personal care, school supplies, and all other expenses. On average, among food-bank users, 18 percent of children and 39 percent of parents go hungry at least once a week in single-parent families with one child, and 45 percent of children and 47 percent of parents do in families with five members. Nevertheless, rent payments are given first priority, to fend off the disaster of homelessness.

In North America, a high proportion of home ownership was made possible by long-term mortgages at relatively low interest rates guaranteed by the central governments of the United States and Canada. For those too poor to benefit from ownership programs, both governments underwrote subsidized housing, called *public housing* in the United States and *assisted housing* in Canada. Both public and assisted housing were badly planned and autocratically and badly run. They were not popular with either taxpayers or tenants. But after these programs were eventually halted or much curtailed, which happens to unpopular programs, waiting lists for spaces grew. In 2002 in Toronto, about 65,000 low-income people were on assisted-housing waiting lists. For nonprofit co-ops, the average wait was five years.

The other part of the shelter equation, the median incomes of families, gradually grew as larger numbers of wives and mothers took paying jobs. Of course, a nuclear family's first response to the radical disconnection between shelter prices and a modest income is to try to make do somehow, short of becoming homeless: cut expenses, find no-cost recreations, take in friends caught in similar difficulties (enlarge the household), procure abortions (limit the household), patronize secondhand stores and yard sales, sell possessions they themselves can spare, and hound governments to hunt down missing fathers who have defaulted on court-ordered child-support payments.

These strategies helped—but not much, because, at the same time, necessary household expenses tended to grow, and not merely because of inflation but because qualitative changes had occurred in what constituted necessary expenses. The most serious and widespread increase was the need for an automobile. Public transportation declined or was altogether absent, especially in suburbs. In cities that underwent urban renewal in the 1950s and later and in new suburbs, stores and working places were segregated from residences, without feasible, much less enjoyable, walking or bicycling routes. By the mid-1960s, simply to get to a job, or to find a job in the first place, or to buy provisions, or to get a child to school or a playground or a playmate, a car became a necessity. Families needed child care while parents were at work and commuting, so from 1970 on, parents followed up leads and chased around to find the limited numbers of subsidized places for children that they could both afford and get to. Inhumanely long car-commutes to work became common enough by 2002 that Canadian police recognized driver drowsiness to be jostling drunken driving as a cause of fatal highway accidents.

Two parents, to say nothing of one, cannot possibly satisfy all the needs of a family-household. A community is needed as well, for raising children, and also to keep adults reasonably sane and cheerful. A community is a complex organism with complicated resources that grow gradually and organically. Its resources fall into three main categories.

First, there are resources that all families need and that virtually none can provide for themselves, nor can any but the largest, richest, and most institutional households provide them. These resources are mostly tangible. They include affordable housing for all the community's members; publicly funded transportation (even privately owned cars need roads, parking lots, and police forces); water and sewage systems; fire protection; public health and safety inspections and enforcement; schools; public libraries; large-scale public recreation facilities; parks; ambulances and other emergency services.

Items in the second category are provided more informally by a community but are also mostly tangible. They consist of convenient and responsive commercial establishments, plus noncommercial (nonprofit) services initiated and maintained by volunteer citizens' groups. These last may, or may not, overlap with publicly provided resources, depending upon differences in government programs and local cultures: for instance, old people's homes and activities; churches or other community gathering centers; concerts, festivals, sports tournaments; language classes; and job training centers.

The third and final category of community resources is thoroughly informal, thoroughly intangible, and probably the most important: speaking relationships among neighbors and acquaintances in addition to friends.

Everyone needs entrées into networks of acquaintances for practical as well as social purposes. Think what the adults in a nuclear family—just the two of them—are expected by society to provide:

Knowledge and experience sufficient to use simple home remedies in cases of trivial illnesses or wounds, and—more important—the ability to judge correctly and quickly when ills or wounds are too serious for home remedies, maybe even life-threatening. Ability to tutor children needing help with homework. Ability to be a soccer mom and a hockey dad. Skill and tact at training children to shun drugs and to be cautious of strangers but not to mistrust everybody. Ability to purchase responsibly, make bill and tax payments, and in general handle money realistically in spite of blandishments to gamble or become profligate. Make ordinary home and equipment repairs and keep abreast of maintenance chores. Deal knowledgeably with banks and bureaucracies. Pull a fair share of family weight in community betterment efforts and neighborhood protection. Deal civilly with people whose upbringing, cultures, and personalities are at odds with the traditions and customs of one's own nuclear family, and teach children to be both cosmopolitan and tolerant. Without this last ability, nuclear families can be irreparably torn asunder when relationships develop between their children and lovers from other ethnic or religious backgrounds or, if the family is very stodgy, simply from other educational or income groups.

Who are the paragons that, unaided and unadvised, can earn a living and also provide all this and more? Few of them exist. Only membership in a functioning community makes handling these responsibilities feasible. Another thing: the neuroses of only two adults (or one) focusing relentlessly on offspring can be unbearable. The diverse viewpoints and strengths of many adults can be educational and liberating. Two adults who have too little adult companionship besides themselves can easily drift into isolation from society and become lonely, paranoid, resentful, stressed, depressed, and at their wits' ends. Sitcom families and "reality" TV can and do fill isolated hours, but cannot offer the support of live friends and the practical information of varied acquaintances.

One can drive today for miles through American suburbs and never glimpse a human being on foot in a public space, a human being outside a car or truck. I have experienced this in suburban Virginia, California, and Massachusetts, as well as suburban Toronto. This is a visible sign that much of North America has become bereft of communities. For communities to exist, people must encounter one another in person. These encounters must include more than best friends or colleagues at work. They must include diverse people who share the neighborhood, and often enough share its needs.

Here is something sad: sometimes an unusually energetic and public-spirited individual in an American or Canadian social desert will start a campaign to improve the place: clean up a trash-filled creek and pond, for instance, or revive a defunct local market and community center. The neighborhood may even receive an award for the achievement. Then what happens? Sometimes the noble idiosyncratic effort lacks staying power; when the originator is lost to aging, death, or relocation, the project fades away, too, because no functioning community exists to carry it on. One of the great strengths of New York City is that its neighborhood community efforts typically have staying power; once under way, they tend to persist not only for decades but for generations. This cultural characteristic, moreover, is perhaps most marked in the densest part of the city, Manhattan.

Not TV or illegal drugs but the automobile has been the chief destroyer of American communities. Highways and roads obliterate the places they are supposed to serve, as, for example, highways feeding the Verrazano-Narrows Bridge wiped out most of the formerly large Bay Ridge community in Brooklyn. Robert Moses, the nearest thing to a dictator with which New York and New Jersey have ever been afflicted (so far), thought of himself as a master builder, and his much diminished corps of admirers still nostalgically recall him as that; but he was a master obliterator. If he had had his way, which he did not because of successful community opposition, one of Manhattan's most vibrant, diverse, and economically productive neighborhoods, SoHo, would have been sacrificed to an expressway. Other forces, acting in concert with automobile culture, have also been pervasive. Along came sterile housing tracts set in isolating culs-de-sac, and shopping centers whose only ties to localities were the dollars of local consumers. These, often enough, erased community hearts and landmarks, as if to make sure that marooned vestiges of what had been lost were also lost.

Of course, many people have opposed what was happening to former communities: thousands upon thousands have poured ingenuity and energy into opposition. Some who are fortunate enough to have communities still do fight to keep them, but they have seldom prevailed. While people possess a community, they usually understand that they can't afford to lose it; but after it is lost, gradually even the memory of what was lost is lost. In miniature, this is the malady of Dark Ages.

If an economist from a neoconservative think tank wants to deny the community destruction wrought, he will probably point out that the American people, through the workings of the free market, decreed the supremacy of the automobile and its public appurtenances and the demise of public transit. Not true. To claim that and be believed is to rely on mass forgetfulness of persistent corporate attacks on public transit for the sake of selling oil, rubber tires, and internal-combustion vehicles. This strategy, led by General Motors' Bus Division, was tested out in a preliminary way in the 1920s on two small cities in Michigan and one in Ohio. The consortium bought electric streetcar lines, demolished them, and replaced them with buses, then resold the lines, tying up the sales with contracts that specified future suppliers of buses, oil, and tires. In the 1930s, with this tactic perfected, scores of transit systems were bought by a General Motors subsidiary called National City Lines. To Depression-stricken cities, the ready money from selling transit systems was irresistible. An electric street-car was more economical to maintain than a bus and lasted three times as long as a bus, so the reconstituted systems were extravagant. Where protesting citizens were well enough informed to be aware of financial disadvantage, other arguments and pressures were brought to bear. In New York, a foolish mayor, Fiorello La Guardia, was convinced by Robert Moses that streetcars were disgracefully old-fashioned. General Motors later awarded Moses $25,000 (about $165,000 in today's money) for an essay on highway planning and financing and gave a generous contribution to the city's World's Fair of 1939, a Moses project.

Belatedly, the antitrust division of the U.S. Department of Justice asked a former judge in Minnesota to investigate what was going on in the rash of transit sales, but with the bombing of Pearl Harbor, the government lost interest in this domestic issue. Sales of electric public-transit systems increased mightily during the war and afterward. National City Lines, together with two additional puppet subsidiaries, by 1950 controlled transit systems in eighty-three cities, among them Los Angeles (whose once extensive and popular web of transit vehicles can be glimpsed in early Hollywood comedies), Philadelphia, Baltimore, San Francisco, Portland (Oregon), Chicago, St. Louis, Salt Lake City, and Tulsa, and many smaller places, such as Montgomery, Alabama.

At the time, New York's decision to convert from trolleys to General Motors buses appeared to have been a major, and perhaps decisive, influence on American communities to come, but in retrospect this wry glory probably belongs instead to the New Jersey suburbs of New York and Philadelphia, where a great web of electric trolley companies, the largest such network in the world at the time, served commuters and tied suburbs together internally and with one another. In 1946, when these highly developed systems (now vanished) were succumbing to the General Motors vision of the world of the future, a former employee wrote from Florida, where he had been serving as a naval commander, to alert hundreds of mayors, city managers, other bureaucrats, and congressmen that they were being "swindled" by "a careful deliberately planned campaign" to obliterate their "most important and valuable public utilities." He asked what is still a good question: "Who will rebuild them for you?"

Again, belatedly, Congress and the Department of Justice took notice. Nine corporations and seven of their executives were indicted for illegal acts in restraint of trade, tried, and convicted. The executives were punished with $1 (yes, one dollar) fines each, and the corporations with $5,000 fines each.

To this day, General Motors persists in attacks on public transit; now the company is targeting electric trolleybuses. In March 2003, General Motors dealers of British Columbia took a full-page advertisement in a Vancouver weekly newspaper, picturing a Vancouver electric bus coming at the reader head-on, identified with a route sign proclaiming WET DOG SMELL. (The only dogs on Vancouver buses are guide dogs accompanying blind passengers.) The following week the bus in the advertisement was identified as a carrier of CREEPS AND WEIRDOS. Both advertisements urged readers to select the alternative: a private General Motors passenger car. General Motors brought upon itself such a deluge of outraged telephone calls and letters that the rest of this prissy campaign was halted—at least temporarily, and at least in Vancouver.

Apologists for General Motors, Firestone Tire, Standard Oil of California, and Phillips Petroleum, and the likes of Moses and La Guardia, maintain that electric public-transit systems would have failed spontaneously owing to competition from jitneys (see note, p. 187). Their contrived failures left taxpayers bearing no end of government subsidies to promote use and accommodation of vehicles. Added to this were the costs borne by hard-pressed individuals and families who could no longer manage without a car. Among the many other economic side effects has been the abandonment of innovative streetcars developed and built during the Great Depression, which, although quieter, faster, more comfortable, and still more durable and economical than previous vehicles, were deprived of markets. Some of these American-developed electric trolleys were still in service in Europe fifty years later. Developed by a committee of transit company presidents, they were called Presidents Committee Cars (PCCs). When Portland, Oregon, bought some recently it had to order them from a manufacturer in the Czech Republic, because the U.S. streetcar manufacturing industry, once the largest and most technologically advanced in the world, no longer exists. One is reminded of how China capriciously jettisoned its ships.

Of course, General Motors, determined though it was, and still is, to force unlimited numbers of gasoline-powered internal-combustion vehicles on America, was not powerful enough to be solely responsible for the highways that have obliterated communities and ensured suburban sprawl. In chapters that follow, I will touch upon other forces, some reaching deep into American cultural traits, that have abetted extreme dependence on private automotive vehicles at the expense of community and family life.

At any time, the destruction of communities to enhance corporations' sales would be a shortsighted cultural trade-off, but the period after World War II, extending into the new millennium, was an especially unfortunate time for this disaster. The erasures of existing communities, and the stillbirths of new ones, coincided with a great migration of peoples within national borders and across them, with massive shifts of families from the land and its incomes to cities and suburbs and their incomes; and from commodity-based production to ingenuity-based production. Never were communities more needed to assimilate and cushion so many unprecedented circumstances, and to help individuals and families make so many adaptations and adjustments.

The collapse of Rome and the onset of its famous Dark Age also coincided with a great migration of peoples. The causes of those migrations differed from those today, but the Romans, too, desperately needed strong communities to assimilate and cushion the many people experiencing unprecedented circumstances, and to help individuals and families adapt and adjust to civilization. The failing and failed Roman communities were not equal to the responsibility and opportunity, though again for reasons that differ from ours.

Most of my observations on North American community loss and other subjects are not news to anyone who takes an interest in the conundrums of our time and is reasonably well fortified against amnesia. Because, as I have already pointed out, whatever significant jolts a culture takes reverberate throughout the culture, I will touch on causes or consequences of community loss again.

If the predicaments of North American families continue mounting and climb further up the income ladder, I have no idea what kinds of households will emerge to deal with needs that families are at a loss to fill. My intuition tells me they will probably be coercive. This is already true of the most swiftly multiplying and rapidly expanding type of American households at the turn of the millennium—prisons.

CHAPTER THREE

Credentialing Versus Educating

In addition to their other major expenses, some North American nuclear families bear the cost of a four-year college or university degree for the family's child or children. The cost has become as necessary as the cost of a car, and for a similar reason: without it, access to a remunerative job is difficult or even impossible.

It has long been recognized that getting an education is effective for bettering oneself and one's chances in the world. But a degree and an education are not necessarily synonymous.

Credentialing, not educating, has become the primary business of North American universities. This is not in the interest of employers in the long run. But in the short run, it is beneficial for corporations' departments of human resources, the current name for personnel departments. People with the task of selecting successful job applicants want them to have desirable qualities such as persistence, ambition, and ability to cooperate and conform, to be a "team player." At a minimum, achieving a four-year university or college degree, no matter in what subject, seems to promise these traits. From the viewpoint of a government agency's or corporation's department of human resources, the institution of higher learning has done the tedious first winnowing or screening of applicants. For the applicant, this means that a résumé without one or more degrees from a respected institution will not be taken seriously enough even to be considered, no matter how able or informed the applicant may be. The credential is not a passport to a job, as naive graduates sometimes suppose. It is more basic and necessary: a passport to consideration for a job.

A degree can also be a passport out of an underclass, or a safety strap to prevent its holder from sinking into an underclass. Without it, as North American high school students are forever being warned, they will be doomed to a work life of "flipping hamburgers." With it, all manner of opportunities may be accessible.

University credentialing thus efficiently combines the services to employers that in simpler and more frugal days were provided by First Class or Eagle rank in the Boy Scouts, and the services to aspiring climbers that in olden days were provided by a College of Heralds with its monopoly on granting the coats of arms that separated their possessors from the underclass. A coat of arms didn't really certify that its possessor could wield a bow or a battle-ax. That wasn't the point.

Students themselves understand perfectly well what they are buying with four years of their youth and associated tuition and living costs. While a degree in some subject has become indispensable, one in a field with a currently promising job market and good pay is thought to be even better; thus student enrollment statistics have become an unofficial appendix to stock market performance. In the summer of 2002, when Internet and other high-tech stocks had gone into the doldrums, *The Washington Post* surveyed enrollment figures in undergraduate computer science departments in the Washington, D.C., area; it reported:

> At Virginia Tech, enrollment of undergraduates in the computer science department will drop 25 percent this year to 300. At George Washington University, the number of incoming freshmen who plan to study computer science fell by more than half this year. . . . In 1997, schools with Ph.D. programs in computer science and computer engineering granted 8,063 degrees. . . . [T]he numbers rose through 2001 when 17,048 [Ph.D.] degrees were awarded. . . . Nine hundred of the 2,000 plus undergraduates studying information technology and engineering at George Mason University were computer science majors last year. This year the enrollment in that major is down to 800, although a newly created and more general information technology major has attracted 200 students. . . . "Having it ease off for a while is a bit of a relief," said a [George Mason] dean. "Particularly with the field as it has been, they don't want to spend four years on something and then not get a job."

The two students whose comments were included in the newspaper's report, apparently as representative of student thinking, advanced somewhat different reasons for shifts from earlier plans. One, who was switching to an unspecified engineering major, said he wanted to do something "more social and more interesting than working with computers. . . . Besides, you can't get the chicks with that anymore." The other, who was switching to business marketing, said, "Technology comes natural to people my age. It's not fascinating anymore." In the meantime, the *Post* reported, the U.S. Department of Labor was contradictorily projecting that "software engineering will be the fastest growing occupation between 2000 and 2010 with other computer-related industries trailing close behind."

All universities possess their own subcultures, and so do departments within universities, varying to the point of being indifferent or even antagonistic to one another, so a generalization cannot describe all accurately. But it is safe to say that credentialing as primary business of institutions of higher learning had gotten under way in the 1960s. Students were the first to notice the change. In the unrest and turbulence of that decade, one thread of complaint came from students who claimed they were shortchanged in education. They had expected more personal rapport with teachers who had become only remote figures in large, impersonal lecture halls. The students were protesting attempts to transmit culture that omitted acquaintance with personal examples and failed to place them on speaking terms with wisdom. In another decade, however, students dropped that cause, apparently taking it for granted that credentialing is the normal primary business of institutions of higher learning and that its cost is an unavoidable initiation fee into acceptable adulthood. If a student takes out a loan to meet the expense, he or she may reach early middle age by the time the loan is paid off. The guarantee behind the loan is the valuable credential itself.

"College degree worth millions, survey finds," my morning paper tells me in July 2002. Every summer for years readers have been given similar tidings, buttressed by statistics, sometimes from government, sometimes from universities themselves. The survey in this case had been made by the U.S. Census Bureau, which reported, the paper said, that "someone whose education does not go beyond high school and who works full time can expect to earn about $1.2 million between ages 25 and 64. . . . Graduating from college and earning advanced degrees translate into higher lifetime earnings: an estimated $4.4 million for doctors, lawyers and others with professional degrees; $2.5 million for college graduates," that is, those with a bachelor's degree.

At this point in the news report, a policy analyst (presumably with a degree to validate the title) working for the American Council on Education, identified as "a higher education advocacy group," chimed in with the moral: "Not all students look at college as an investment, but I'm sure their parents do. The challenge is to convince those high school students on the margins that it is really worth their time to go to college."

The survey found that men with professional degrees may expect to earn almost $2 million more than "women with the same level of education," a difference attributed to the time out that women take to bear and rear infants.

The trends in the United States have followed in Canada, with the usual time lag. A forum panelist in Toronto, asked by a troubled parent, "When did we decide to change the way we thought about public education?" replied in an essay published in 2003: "Today's youngsters have had it drummed into their heads that a post-secondary education is the key to a good job. . . . [It] is no longer considered as an investment that society makes in the next generation; it is seen as an investment that students make in themselves." The panelist/essayist assigned the start of the Canadian change to the late 1980s, tracing it as a decline then and through the 1990s in public funding to universities and colleges while their enrollments were growing from 15 percent of high school graduates in 1975 to 20 percent in 2001, with educators and legislators expecting that it will reach 25 percent in the near future.

Expansion of first-rate faculty—memorable teachers of the kind the 1960s student protesters were mourning—has not kept pace with expansion of enrollments and courses offered; professors lack the time and energy they could once devote to personal contact with students. Slack has been taken up by what became known as "gypsy faculty," lecturers hoping for permanent appointments as they move from university to university, and by graduate students as part of their apprenticeships. So many papers to mark, relative to numbers and qualities of mentors to mark them, changed the nature of test papers. Some came to consist of "True or false?" and "Which of the following is correct?" types of questions, fit for robots to answer and to rate, rather than stimulants and assessments of critical thinking and depth of understanding.

In the meantime, rejoicing that university education has become a growth industry, administrators and legislators seek increasingly to control problems of scale by applying lessons from profit-making enterprises that turn expanded markets to advantage by cutting costs. Increased output of product can be measured more easily as numbers of credentialed graduates than as numbers of educated graduates. Quantity trumps quality.

Community colleges that grant two-year diplomas in applied arts and sciences represent a midstation in life, like a second-class ticket in the traditional European transportation arrangement of first and second classes and third class or steer-age. Two-year community colleges supply the economy with technicians of many kinds for hospitals and clinics, draftsmen for architectural and engineering firms, designers of graphics, lighting, and costumes for television shows, expositions, and plays, and many, many other skilled workers and craftsmen. Community colleges have typically maintained an admirably close connection between education and training and the diploma credential. But this, too, is now on the verge of a transformation into credentialing disconnected from educa-tion. In my home province of Ontario, Canada, a few com-munity colleges have already promoted themselves into "an elite level" by gaining government licenses to grant four-year degrees that will upstage diplomas. The push for this change came from community college administrators, although they were divided about its desirability. Some feared it would "compromise access." One, who applauded it, argued that his institution has needed a degree-granting license "in order for our college to compete in a sophisticated economy where a degree is the currency of the realm."

To put it crassly, first-class elite-level tickets cost more than second-class tickets. "Undergrad Tuition Fees up 135% over 11 Years," shouts a headline over a 2002 analysis by Statistics Canada, the country's census bureau. Cuts have caused govern-ment funding to fall far behind fifteen years of compounded in-flation. Appended to the newspaper report of the cost increases was a comment by the chair of a national student federation, who noted, "It's no longer just the poorest of the poor who are denied. It's creeping up the income ladder."

As currency of the realm, credentials are attractive to coun-terfeiters. So it is not surprising to learn that "experts" (credentials unspecified) estimate that 30 percent of job applicants concoct false résumés, and that a former mayor of San Francisco, when told that his chief of police had lied about his college degrees, pooh-poohed the revelation with the comment, "I don't know who doesn't lie on their resumes." It is surprising, however, to learn that captains of industry give in to the temptation. After an unsuccessful career as an executive at General Motors, the successful chief executive of Bausch & Lomb, a venerable and respected maker of lenses and other eye-care products, was shown not to possess a master of business administration degree, as claimed in his biographical materials. His competence was affirmed by his corporation's board, and neither he nor the company suffered from the revelation except for a sharp but temporary drop in the company's stock. Other executives have been less fortunate. The chief executive of Veritas Software was fired for falsely claiming an MBA from Stanford University, and others have been publicly embarrassed. One told the press, "At some point I probably felt insecure and it perpetuated itself." The Bausch & Lomb president, standing on his dignity, wins the arm's-length prize: "I'm embarrassed," he told the press, "that some of this incorrect information appeared in some of our published materials on my background. Clearly, it's my obligation to proof-read such things carefully and ensure their accuracy."

Credentialing is an indirect legacy of the Great Depression of the 1930s. Along with much else in North American culture, credentialing's origins and appeal cannot be understood without harking back to the Depression years.

The physical and financial hardships of America in the years 1930–39 were mild in comparison with hardships endured in

the twentieth century by societies that suffered famine, genocide, ethnic cleansing, oppression, bombing raids, or defeat in
war. The Depression, however, exerted a lasting influence on
Americans, out of all proportion to its short duration and relatively mild ordeals. Nobody understood what was happening when jobs and savings vanished and stagnation settled on
the United States and Canada. Even now, some seventy years
later, economists continue to dispute the Depression's causes.
Mass unemployment was the single greatest disaster. At its
worst, it idled some 25 percent of workers in the United States
and Canada, and higher percentages in hard-hit localities.
When one considers all the others who directly and indirectly
depended on those workers, unemployment or its effects
touched almost everyone other than the exceptionally rich or
sheltered. Government make-work and semi-welfare programs, some of them admirably ingenious and constructive,
helped but did not cure, and they had their own insecurities
and humiliations.

Some people spent most of the Depression years standing
in lines for a chance at a temporary job, for delayed pay from
bankrupt companies, for lost savings in failed banks, for bowls
of soup or loaves of day-old bread. One sees the anxious rows
of pinched faces in photographs of the time. Also in photographs one sees rallies of protesters with their signs, quailing
before mounted police and raised billy clubs. Often with in-
credible bravery, and always with incalculable expenditures of
time, scrimped savings, and hopes, protesters devoted themselves to political activities that they had convinced themselves
would be beneficial. Quieter involvement with intellectual
schemes, like technocracy, social credit, and EPIC (End Poverty
in California, the platform of Upton Sinclair's unsuccessful

campaign for election as that state's governor), was a comfort to many. Others busied themselves politically with combat against those who espoused Marxism, Trotskyism, or other radical politics. Some of these, too, and their opponents turn up in photographs of sessions of the U.S. House of Representatives Un-American Activities Committee.

However, most attempts at living through the Depression are not documented in photographs at all; they were only very lightly touched on in films, and almost as lightly in music. People who weren't used to being idle and unwanted tried to keep busy somehow; but even jobs at no pay, valued for learning and experience, were hard to get. Architects made jigsaw puzzles and renderings of ghastly, inhuman utopian cities and sold them if customers could be found. I got a job without pay, for a year, on the Scranton, Pennsylvania, morning paper. The editor needed another reporter but lacked money to hire one. I earned his staff's generous tutoring by producing news items and articles the paper used. Although the paper was unionized (Scranton had the second Newspaper Guild local in the United States), nobody objected to my Depression make-do barter agreement.

For individuals, the worst side effect of unemployment was repeated rejection, with its burden of shame and failure. Many quietly despaired that the world had a place for them. This hopelessness, at the time, seemed endless. Would life always be like this? Something unfathomable, without visible cause, had engulfed everyone's expectations and plans.

For someone in her teens or early twenties, as I was during the Depression decade, it wasn't really so bad. My friends and I could make stories out of our rejections and frugalities and the strange people we met up with in our futile searches and could bask in the gasps or laughs we generated. It was harder for people in their thirties, who had gotten launched (they thought) in careers that so soon came to nothing. For people in their forties or fifties, rejections and idleness could be devastating. The parents of some of my friends never recovered ease with themselves, their families, or society after this demoralizing break in their lives. It was harder on men who had been family breadwinners than on women who devoted themselves to homemaking and child rearing, as most did after marriage.

My father, a doctor, worked long hours, seven days a week, and in spite of weariness he stayed in good spirits because he was needed and, especially, because his work interested him. But, like everyone else, he worried about getting by. In our little city, where the chief industry was mining expensive, high-grade anthracite coal, the Great Depression was intensified because, in effect, it had started four years early with a long and bitter coal strike and subsequent loss of markets.

Few of my father's patients were able to pay him, as the effects of mass unemployment spread. He told me one Saturday evening in 1936 that he had to earn $48 a day merely to pay for his office rent, his subscriptions to medical journals, office supplies, and the salary of his assisting nurse. To me that seemed an incomprehensibly formidable sum; I was earning $12 a week in New York as a stenographer in a candy manufacturing company that soon went into bankruptcy. He expressed relief that that day he had broken even, thanks to twelve hours of hard, concentrated work in his office and the hospitals where he was a visiting physician and surgeon. He was not unique. Countless Americans who thought of themselves as the backbone of the country kept doing their work regardless of the struggle and helped hold things together.

When the stagnation lifted, at first tentatively in 1938–39 as the armament economy clicked in, and then in full force in 1942 after America entered the war, the change was miraculous. It was too late for my father, who had died in 1937. Everyone knew it was ghoulish to delight in jobs and prosperity at the price of war; nevertheless, everyone I knew was grateful that suddenly good jobs and pay raises showered like rain after a drought. It seemed that the world did need us, and had places for us.

After the war was over, during the euphoria of victory and the minor booms of the Marshall Plan and the Korean War, a consensus formed and hardened across North America. If it had been voiced, it would have gone something like this: *"We can endure meaningful trials and overcome them. But never again— never, never—will we suffer the meaningless disaster of mass unemployment."*

Cultures take purposes for themselves, cling tenaciously to them, and exalt them into the purposes and meanings of life itself. For instance, in ancient Rome the ideal of service to the state was the overriding cultural purpose. After the republic was succeeded by the empire, Virgil added a slightly new spin, in a passage of the *Aeneid* cited with reverence by the emperor Augustus: "Your task, Roman, is this: to rule the peoples. This is your special genius: to enforce the habits of peace, to spare the conquered, to subdue the proud."

In medieval Western Europe and in early colonial Puritan America, the purpose of life, which had been reshaped during the Dark Age, became the salvation of souls, one's own and others', for the Christian Kingdom of Heaven.

In the founding period of the United States, a time when the Copernican, Newtonian, and Cartesian Enlightenment had succeeded both medievalism and the Renaissance, the cultural purpose became independence. Not for nothing was the charter of reasons behind the war of separation from Britain called the Declaration of Independence, and July Fourth called Independence Day. An accompanying cult developed around liberty, as symbolized by both the Liberty Bell and the aims of the French Revolution. Independence and liberty were succeeded by the related freedom, indeed by two conflicting versions of freedom: the political freedom of states' rights, offshoot of independence, and the social freedom of abolition of slavery, offshoot of liberty.

In the decades after the Civil War, and the bloodletting that seemed briefly to resolve the conflict between concepts of freedom, there was no obvious American cultural consensus on the purpose of life, although there were contenders, such as the Manifest Destiny of America's push westward, which had already risen to its height in the 1840s with the Mexican War, the annexation of Texas, and the purchase of California and New Mexico. Manifest Destiny was extended at the turn of the century by President Theodore Roosevelt to the Caribbean and the Pacific with the Spanish-American War, which was taken by Americans to mean American rule over the Western Hemisphere.

The start of the twentieth century and the decades immediately before and after were a time of reforming ferment as Americans sought to perfect their society by eliminating child labor, extending the vote to women, combating corruption and fraud, embracing public health measures and their enforcement, prohibiting the sale of alcohol, outlawing monopolies as restraints on trade, initiating environmental conservation through national parks (a favorite of Theodore Roosevelt's), improving working conditions and protecting the rights of labor, and pursuing many other practical reforms into which their proponents threw themselves with ardor as great as if each of these aims were indeed the purpose of life.

The reforming spirit carried into the Great Depression years, with President Franklin Roosevelt's promotion of the Four Freedoms, linking economic aims (freedom from want) to human rights (freedom from fear) and his practical measures for making the links tangible, among them his successful advocacy of collective bargaining under the Robert F. Wagner proposals that became the National Labor Relations Act, and his institution of a regulatory Securities and Exchange Commission (SEC), making rules for public corporations' disclosures and reining in speculative manipulations in corporate stocks. Eleanor Roosevelt, Franklin's wife, for her part, channeled her lifelong experience with smallish reform movements into advocacy of the United Nations and, most notably, into that body's formulation and acceptance of a declaration of universal human rights, her chief legacy and monument. Among all these and other contenders for the American purpose of life, one seemed to win out, less with fanfare than with simple quiet acceptance: the American dream, the ideal that each generation of whites, whether immigrant or native-born, was to become more successful and prosperous than the parent generation.

From the 1950s on, American culture's gloss on the purpose of life became assurance of full employment: jobs. Arguably, this has remained the American purpose of life, in spite of competition from the Cold War with the Soviet Union, and maybe even from the War on Terrorism, in which postwar reconstruction was linked with contracts for American companies and hence jobs for Americans.

How does a culture reveal its concept of the purpose of life? A cultural purpose enables perpetrators and witnesses to regard horrific deeds as righteous. Republican Rome's defeat of Carthage and its people—Virgil's cant notwithstanding—was as gruesome a murder scene of helpless and innocent people as has been recorded; it was deemed glorious by Romans because they construed it as a righteous act of preemptive protection for the state. Looting and massacres by sixteenth-century Spanish conquistadores in South and Central America were justified by the same cultural drives for salvation of souls that justified the labors, sacrifices, and risks of Spanish missionaries. The aggressions of crusading soldiers and kings against Muslim "infidels" in the Middle East and Christian heretics in France; the tortures and executions in Europe by Catholic inquisitors and Protestant witch-hunters; the persecutions and forced conversions of Jews; the oppressions by Puritans in Britain and New England—these and other deeds that created hell on earth were all righteously justified as defeats of the devil and salvation of souls.

In 1956, when Congress passed legislation funding the Interstate Highway System—a government program then unprecedented in America for its vast physical scope and vast cost—the ostensible reason for the program was to allow residents and workers to evacuate cities and towns speedily and efficiently in case of emergency (a Roman type of purpose). However, memories of the Great Depression were sufficiently fresh for everyone to recognize instantly the real and serious purpose of the program: full employment; guarantee of jobs: jobs building roads, jobs designing, manufacturing, servicing, and repairing automobiles, jobs refining and transporting oil and filling gasoline tanks. President Dwight D. Eisenhower himself acknowledged this purpose in his remarks about the automobile as a mainstay of the economy and employment, when he spoke at the George Washington Bridge in New York at a celebration as the highway program was getting under way.

To settle on the auto industry as the instrument for achieving jobs, the grand cultural purpose of life, was so apt that it may have been all but inevitable. Automobiles, for those who could afford them, were loaded with references and romances from earlier American purposes and meanings of life: independence, freedom, the success of getting a better car than one's parents could afford—moving up from a Pontiac to a Buick. Nobody recognized and approved the job-making purpose of the highway system more heartily than mayors and other elected officials. The shortsighted destruction of community in America was easily trumped by the righteousness of full employment.

Conflicts between highway building and community values—or any other values—set a pattern that has persisted after memories of the Great Depression have faded. To foreigners, it seems inconsistent that America promotes globalization of trade, yet also gives subsidies to American agriculture that sorely hurt poor African economies; claps tariffs on Canadian sawn lumber and Brazilian steel, and sets quotas on imports of Chinese textiles. To American trade negotiators and lobbyists, however, there is no inconsistency in contradictory policies that, each in its own way, are calculated to promote jobs for Americans. What is inconsistent about that?

Any institution, including a government agency, that is bent upon ecological destruction or an outrage on the built environment argues its case or bullies its opponents by righteously citing the jobs that supposedly will materialize or, even more effectively, the jobs that may be forfeited or jeopardized if the ugly deed is not done. To this day, no alternative disaster, including possible global warming, is deemed as dire a threat as job loss. At a time in 2002 when Canada's Arctic was unmistakably melting—and unexpectedly rapidly, too—the premier of Ontario was asked whether he would support the Canadian prime minister in his professed intent to ratify the Kyoto accord on reduction of climate-warming fossil-fuel emissions or would instead follow the lead of U.S. president George W. Bush in repudiating the accord. His reply: "We're not going to put ourselves at a huge disadvantage and cost Ontarians hundreds of thousands of jobs . . . while our American neighbors to the south—God bless them—are not doing something about reducing their emissions."

That is the Great Depression speaking, on both sides of the border. As exalted cultural purposes of life go, a job for everyone is less brutal and deluded than most cultural ideals. But, as my grandmother used to say, "You can run anything into the ground."

Whether jobs have been succeeded by the War on Terrorism as the American purpose of life is still unclear. The swift surrender of entitlement to a speedy trial, protection against being held without legal counsel or charges, and privacy, and, in the case of captured combatants, the abrogation of the Geneva Conventions on treatment of prisoners of war, argue that the exigencies of outmaneuvering putative terrorists have overridden other values, including economic prudence. As Margaret Atwood has pointed out, the surrender of civil rights is "a recipe for widespread business theft . . . and fraud." Perhaps we must wait for new arrangements for control of Middle Eastern oil and reconstruction of Afghanistan and Iraq to learn whether the purpose of American life has actually switched from providing jobs and earning profits.

It has been truly said that the past lives on in the present.

This is true of credentialism's origins. It emerged partly out of America's humiliation and worry when the Soviet Union, with its Sputnik, had beaten America into space, and partly from the still-fresh dread of the Depression. Credentialism emerged, mostly in California at first, in the late 1950s, when it dawned upon university administrators there that modern economic development, whether in the conquest of space or any other field, depended on a population's funds of knowledge—a resource that later came to be known as human capital. It followed that development's most culturally valuable product—jobs—also depended on knowledge. The administrators were quite right, and it was brainy of them to reason that the more of this crucial resource their institutions could nurture and certify, the better for all concerned.

Initially there was no conflict between this aim and the quality of the education that administrators expected their institutions to supply. That conflict began to arise in the 1960s, partly out of universities' attempts to take on many new tasks at once, as they engaged with the communities that supported them. Under the civic banner of the "multiversity" they aimed at furthering every good thing they set their abundant intellects to. Far from elevating credentialing above educating, they were sweepingly enlarging the idea of educating to embrace whatever skills seemed needed, from cost-benefit analysis to marketing. Administrators surely did not recognize how much these enlarged ambitions, coupled with the promise of riches to society from credentialed graduates, would change universities themselves.

As always in a culture, everything that happened connected with much else. In this case, multiversity educational expansion had connections with a constructive U.S. government program for war veterans.

After World War II and then the Korean War, the government provided tuition and encouragement for veterans who had the desire and qualifications to attend universities or colleges. Tens of thousands of former GIs, many from families in which nobody had ever before been given a chance at higher education, took advantage of this opportunity. On the whole, the veterans were noted for applying themselves more seriously than students just out of high school. They also swelled student enrollments. When the stream of GI students ran dry, their hunger for education was missed in university communities, along with their government-guaranteed tuitions. Credentialing emerged as a growth industry in the 1960s just when universities needed it to address problems of their own.

The more successful credentialing became as a growth industry, the more it dominated education, from the viewpoints of both teachers and students. Teachers could not help despairing of classes whose members seemed less interested in learning than in doing the minimum work required to get by and get out. Enthusiastic students could not help despairing of institutions that seemed to think of them as raw material to process as efficiently as possible rather than as human beings with burning questions and confusions about the world and doubts about why they were sinking time and money into this prelude to their working lives.

Students who are passionate about learning, or could become so, do exist. Faculty members who love their subjects passionately and are eager to teach what they know and to plumb its depths further also exist. But institutions devoted to respecting and fulfilling these needs as their first purposes have become rare, under pressure of different necessities. Similar trends in Britain have begun to worry some educators there. My impression is that university-educated parents or grandparents of students presently in university do not realize how much the experience has changed since their own student days, nor do the students themselves, since they have not experienced anything else. Only faculty who have lived through the loss realize what has been lost.

A vigorous culture capable of making corrective, stabilizing changes depends heavily on its educated people, and especially upon their critical capacities and depth of understanding. Most parts of North America have already become backward in production and distribution of renewable forms of energy. As for the continent's cherished automobile and roads industries, how stagnant they are! For decades, improvements in automobile manufacturing and design have come from elsewhere, notably Japan and Germany. Changes to combat the wastes of suburban sprawl and lack of suburban communities don't come at all, in spite of much talk and hand-wringing; neither do solutions to city traffic problems, subjects I shall touch on in the next chapter. They, too, are connected with credentialism at the expense of education.

CHAPTER FOUR

Science Abandoned

In North America, science is admired almost to the point of worship. It is easy to understand why. Science and its offspring, science-based technology, have lengthened and lightened the human life span. Science has enriched our acquaintance with our planet: revealed its geological history, instructed us in the life the planet supports, cautioned us about its vulnerabilities and the protection we owe it, and clarified the interdependence of its parts.

To be sure, science is also mistrusted by those who don't like its discoveries for religious, political, ethical, or even esthetic reasons. Some thoughtful people complain that science has erased enchantment from the world. They have a point. Miracles, magic, and other fascinating impossibilities are no longer much encountered except in movies. But in the light shed by the best science and scientists, everything is fascinating, and the more so the more that is known of its reality. To science, not even the bark of a tree or a drop of pond water is dull or a handful of dirt banal. They all arouse awe and wonder.

Science doesn't supply happiness; but neither does its lack. The same can be said of social utopias: they aren't created by science, but neither does lack of science provide them. Science has cast up dangerous and cruel knowledge, which has been exploited for warfare and dictatorial power; but so have cultures so little gifted with scientists that they either make do with imported weapons or rely on clubs, axes, and daggers. Scientific information about our mistakes—for instance, that deforestation invites mud slides and deserts, that overfishing depletes fish stocks—doesn't guarantee we will avoid such mistakes or correct them, but that is owing to failure to heed what science uncovers.

Despite all of science's shortcomings as a source of perfection, it still remains that the wealth, well-being, and creative power of our culture, and increasingly of South and East Asia as well, depend heavily on science and technology.

What is this valuable thing? It isn't a thing but a state of mind. Its aim is to get at truths about how reality works. However, that aim in itself does not distinguish science from spying, guessing, and using analogies, which also, with less success than science, aim at discovering truths. The scientific pursuit of truth uses no end of tools, ranging from sensitive scales able to register the weight of a hair to observatories of the heavens.

Science is distinguished from other pursuits by the precise and limited intellectual means that it employs and the integrity with which it uses its limited means. The standard description of the scientific state of mind outlines four steps or stages, beginning with a fruitful question.

Science constantly builds further upon truths it has already bagged. Each further discovery starts anew with its own fruitful question. "Fruitful" means that the question must take into account, as far as possible, everything already known about the object, event, or process under scrutiny and, amid this richness of information, must single out a salient mystery or obscurity. This is harder than it sounds, because salient mysteries are apt to be overlooked or taken for granted. Examples from the past could be: "How does water get up into clouds?" and "How does blood from the feet get up to the heart?" Each of these questions, in its own context, was splendidly fruitful. I have mischievously coupled them here to suggest how misleading analogies can be.

After fruitful questions are answered, the answers themselves dispose of false analogies: for instance, what an absurdity to suppose that evaporation does the work of leg veins' valves, or vice versa. Yet as we shall see, slovenly use of analogies is one pitfall of some North American science.

Equipped with a fruitful question, the scientist frames a hypothetical answer, accounting as elegantly and economically as possible—"parsimoniously" is the word favored—for the truth that he or she suspects is hiding behind the question. The question, and the hypothetical answer, together constitute two closely linked stages that require insight, imagination, and courage, qualities possessed by all creative scientists, and in high degree by scientific geniuses.

In the third stage, the hypothesis is tested, by both its creator and others. Ultimately, the real world tests all hypotheses, and usually quickly. When answers from the real world seem to come slowly, it is seldom the evidence itself that is slow to appear; rather, observers are blind to evidence or emotionally can't bear to credit it. This is why the crashing of the Berlin Wall finally was required as an exclamation point, after unheeded evidence of many decades reported that Marxism was untruthful as an economic theory. An example from medicine is the discovery that peptic ulcers are caused by bacteria, not psychological stress; for years, the evidence assembled by an Australian doctor was ignored by other specialists.

Deliberate tests of a hypothesis can often be contrived experimentally. Tests contrived in the laboratory, like those coming in unsought from life, are useless in the absence of observers alert to evidence, or in the presence of observers who lack respect for evidence. Wishful thinking absolutely does not do. If a hypothesis stands up well to assault by testing, it is eventually accepted as theory or even law, as in "the law of gravity" or "the laws of perspective."

In its fourth and final stage, a successful hypothesis opens up questions previously not even known to exist. For instance, a theory that cholera epidemics spread from contaminated drinking water—a startling finding by John Snow, a nineteenth-century London physician who noticed a correspondence between incidence of cases and a district in the city that was served by a specific well—opened up the sequel question, "How does drinking water become contaminated by cholera as an infectious agent?" The answer, "Sewage," opened up still further questions. Copernicus's stupendous theory that the earth revolves around the sun opened up many other questions, such as "What holds the earth to its course?"

This fourth stage, the question chain, sustains science as a coherent process, erecting continuous, coherent bodies of knowledge. Thus science itself, rather than the will of scientists or the judgments of patrons and grant givers, directs its own organization, along with providing automatic and continual self-renewal. New questions turning up in the question chain, especially if they are a surprise, return the entire process to its first stage: again, the time is ripe to pose a salient and fruitful question.

In this account, I have idealized the process by making it appear tidier than it usually is. Earlier, I called science-based technology the offspring of science. It would be quite as truthful to speak of technology-based science as the offspring of technology.

Discovering truth, when the process is initiated with technology, often begins with the question "How?" rather than "Why?" or even "What?" Louis Pasteur's great question "How can wine be protected from spoiling during fermentation?" and the further questions opened up underlie all bacteriological knowledge.

"How can we get water power to drive a boat?" "How can the power of steam drive a machine?" "How can the actions of the machine direct and control the actions of the steam?" "How do the egg and the sperm together create the plant's heredity?" "How do losing cultures lose?"

Questions like these employ the same state of mind as the idealized procedure I sketched out. The main difference is a matter of timing among the stages. In "How?" questions, which are often technology driven, the hypothesis is apt to come *after* experiments and evidence, and to be formed by results of the experiments and evidence (often in many substages of investigation and correction) as much as by an original question. Along the way, many minor insights may be contributed, instead of one grand, major insight. A hypothesis formed at a late stage of a project can be quite as grand as one that takes the lead—and can be a major surprise too, not having been an answer consciously sought in advance.

Late-forming hypotheses tend to make use of feedback, an information process analyzed by mid-twentieth-century computer scientists. Feedback is now understood and valued as essential to dynamic systems, conspicuously including ecological and biochemical systems and early childhood neurological development; feedback is so essential in these systems that if it halts or malfunctions, the whole system dies or otherwise fails. In science, feedback is evidence.

In sum, the scientific state of mind works along two slightly different avenues, one abstract, the other feeling its way more concretely and pragmatically. Both approaches demand integrity, awareness of evidence and respect for it, and attention to new questions that arise as immediate practical problems to be grappled with, or else as more abstract and postponable. Both avenues are valid and effective. They work together so well that they frequently shift back and forth in the course of an investigation, or they overlap.

If a body of inquiry becomes disconnected from the scientific state of mind, that unfortunate segment of knowledge is no longer scientific. It stagnates. Intellectually, it is poisonous, because thereafter almost everything the stagnated and warped knowledge touches is harmed by it. Nazi ideologies of race, Marxist ideologies of economics and social utopias, capitalist confusion of commercial competition with Darwinism, along with the elimination of cooperation from understanding of evolution, are all examples of inquiries claiming scientific validity that were disconnected from the scientific state of mind and sank into dogma.

Thomas Kuhn, a twentieth-century historian of science,

has pointed out that previously established scientific verities are themselves capable of hampering scientific advancement. He called such verities paradigms and drew attention to the fact that they shape people's entire worldviews. Most people do not enjoy having their entire worldview discredited; it sets them uncomfortably adrift. Scientists are no exception. A paradigm tends to be so greatly cherished that, as new knowledge or evidence turns up that contradicts it or calls it into question, the paradigm is embroidered with qualifications and exceptions, along with labored pseudo-explanations—anything, no matter how intellectually disreputable or craven, to avoid losing the paradigm. If a paradigm is truly obsolete, it must finally give way, discredited by the testing of the real world. But outworn paradigms ordinarily stand staunchly until somebody within the field makes a leap of insight, imagination, and courage sufficient to dislodge the obsolete paradigm and replace it.

The scientific state of mind is a major marvel in its own right. Sometimes it slips up, either in the interest of preserving an unfit paradigm or because it has fallen asleep. These lapses are not as nefarious as betrayals of science that are motivated by greed or pursuit of power, but nevertheless they are dangerous, perhaps the more so because they do not necessarily signal their dishonesty with obviously ugly immorality. The enemy of truth is untruth, whatever its motivation. Even high-minded "scientific" untruth always exacts costs, and often they are large and ramified beyond all preliminary calculation.

I am now going to relate a few illustrative instances in which the scientific state of mind has been betrayed and science abandoned, while those carrying out the ugly deeds pretend that nothing of the kind has happened and perhaps do not realize themselves what they have done, since they have probably lost the memory of the state of mind they have lost.

My first example is a lapse in a minor branch of engineering known as traffic engineering or traffic management. It is a lapse of practical importance because it wastes the time of many drivers, contributes to pollution, wastes land and energy, and is the most active single cause of community destruction discussed in Chapter 2.

Engineering has an honorable and long pedigree as a science. Most of the sporadic evidences of a scientific state of mind that go back to time immemorial are revealed by feats of engineering. In part, this is owing to the solidity and durability of such achievements as the Roman aqueducts, the pyramids in Egypt and in what is now Latin America, and the domes, arches, and seawalls of classical construction. Today our safety is constantly in the keeping of structural engineers, aeronautical engineers, electrical engineers, chemical engineers, mechanical engineers, hydraulic engineers, and nuclear engineers. We trust the scientific integrity of these people. If we didn't, we'd go crazy. Many branches of civil engineering owe their starts to military engineering in the service of mounting sieges or withstanding them. This military strand in the pedigree has contributed to the profession a proud touch of unstinting, responsible, and even heroic service.

Given this enviable professional background, plus the extreme tendency of North Americans to admire scientific achievement and give it the benefit of the doubt, it is little wonder that traffic engineers have been trusted to do pretty much as they please, and that departments of public works have gratefully accepted and followed their recommendations for design and specifications of streets and roads.

In what traffic engineers have chosen to do and have recommended, they have abandoned and betrayed science as it is understood. "Engineering" also has an opprobrious connotation of manipulation without regard for truth, as in "engineering consensus," or "It looked spontaneous, but it was engineered." It is popularly assumed that when universities give science degrees in traffic engineering, as they do, they are recognizing aboveboard expert knowledge. But they aren't. They are perpetrating a fraud upon students and upon the public when they award credentials in this supposed expertise.

In the mid-1950s, I was one among thousands of New York citizens trying to save Washington Square, the major Greenwich Village community park, from bisection by a limited-access expressway, or reduction to a traffic circle by a circumferential expressway. After staving off both these threats in sequence, our community movement discarded its defensive stance and insisted aggressively that a two-lane carriage road bisecting the square be closed to all but emergency traffic such as ambulances and fire trucks. We now saw that this formerly harmless relic of the horse-and-buggy age was a potential Trojan horse that could be trotted out as a precedent for any kind of road ruination of the park and community.

When a test closing of the carriage road became imminent, the traffic commissioner told us that traffic is like water: if it is dammed up or diverted from its course in one place, it will find other outlets where it meets less resistance. To close off the carriage road without providing a new road would, he predicted, inundate all the narrow streets in the park's vicinity with thwarted traffic and belching fumes, threatening the safety of children to the point that they couldn't even reach the park. He predicted that we would come back to him on our knees, begging for a road.

His dire predictions did not come true. Nowhere did traffic increase. Indeed, traffic counts were slightly down in the park's vicinity. The test closing was so successful that, without more ado, it was made permanent.

Where did the vanished traffic go? This was a new question that emerged unexpectedly. But it was not pursued. It was ignored in favor of a vague notion that some drivers must have chosen less frustrating routes, or else switched to public transit; or maybe some oddballs walked.

More than thirty years later, my Toronto neighborhood was divided over the question of how to frustrate drivers who, to avoid the traffic lights on a main street, used a parallel quiet street as a speedway, zipping unhindered by traffic lights through intersections. Some residents wanted to thwart those drivers by changing the direction of the quiet street (from one-way north to one-way south) on a block partway up the route. Other residents, perhaps a majority, feared that thwarted traffic would inundate their nearby streets. Some wanted nothing done, supposing that any attempted remedies would make matters worse. Still others advocated elaborate and expensive studies of possible traffic mazes throughout the community; others were chastened by the unfortunate experiences of a nearby neighborhood for which an elaborate professional study had been done, leaving everyone dissatisfied. People were getting very angry at one another. Accusatory petitions were bouncing around. Staff members of the city's traffic and public works departments were present at a neighborhood meeting to offer advice. Our local elected council member was present, keeping his ear to the ground.

To my astonishment, as the meeting got under way, I heard from the professional staff the same lecture, almost word for word, that I had heard three decades earlier in New York: that traffic is like water and will find an outlet offering less resistance. If it is diverted or dammed it will inundate other streets.

I thought sadly, "Here they are, another generation of nice, miseducated young men, about to waste their careers in a fake science that cares nothing about evidence; that doesn't ask a fruitful question in the first place and that, when unexpected evidence turns up anyhow, doesn't pursue it; a science that hasn't been building up a coherent body of knowledge that organizes its own direction by grace of the succession of questions it opens." Fortunately, the public present at the meeting cared about evidence. I described what had happened at Washington Square, and the community agreed to test a change in street direction. The professional staff made it clear they didn't like this decision, but the local councilman picked up the idea of the test and apparently overruled the credentialed professionals.

Much the same thing happened as in New York. I don't know whether total traffic counts dropped. No counts were evidently made, or at least reported. But no other streets were inundated by thwarted traffic, and speeding traffic wonderfully decreased on the rescued street, on which I live. It seemed to decrease throughout the neighborhood. Dammed traffic did not overflow into channels of less resistance; it was successfully confined to its appointed channel. Again, the water hypothesis to explain traffic flow had been discredited by the real world. But once again, reasons why it was wrong were not investigated.

However, at long last, other people in the world noticed that unexpected evidence was turning up. My brother, a retired chemical engineer, sent me a clipping from the February 16, 1998, issue of *Chemical & Engineering News* about a study reported in *The New Scientist*. A research team at University College, London, had analyzed—for London Transport and Britain's Department of the Environment, Transport, and the Regions—sixty cases, worldwide, in which roads had been closed or their carrying capacity reduced. The principal finding of the study was forthrightly reported:

> Planners' models assume that closing a road causes the traffic using it to move elsewhere. . . . The study team . . . found that computer models used by urban transportation planners yield incorrect answers. . . . [W]hen a road is closed, an average of 20% of the traffic it carried seems to vanish. In some cases they studied, as much as 60% of the traffic vanished. Most of the cases studied involved urban areas, but the same arguments may apply away from urban areas, *New Scientist* reports. The report at hand is a logical extension to a 1994 finding that building new roads generates traffic. If that's the case, "then the closure of roads is bound to cause less traffic," according to London-based transport consultant Keith Buchan.

The item added, mentioning no further investigation or evidence, that "traffic vanishes because commuting habits are so variable. . . . Flexibility helps people cope with road closures. . . . Experts . . . suggest that government should stop worrying about causing vehicular congestion by pedestrianizing sites."

Thwarted drivers again, making choices. How do traffic engineers know that, or think that they do? This incurious profession pulls its conclusions about the meaning of evidence out of thin air—sheer guesswork—even when it does deign to notice evidence. By the time I read this clipping, I had begun to wonder whether missing traffic—meaning cars and their occupants—actually did vanish or if, instead, only some of their traveling on the roads vanished. The repeated phenomenon of vanished traffic suggested that possibly some characteristics common to the closed roads themselves, rather than the drivers on the roads, might account for vanished traffic. Not an answer to the mystery, but perhaps worth investigating.

I am in no position to do traffic research. I don't drive, nor do I own a car. I have no little cables that will register each time a car runs over their piece of roadway. In recent years I have had a disability that prevents me from walking a distance. When I go to a destination in downtown Toronto, I take a taxi. But, as luck would have it, a taxi has turned out to be an admirable tool for helping me indulge my curiosity.

When I travel from the airport to a downtown microdestination, one part of the trip can be along an elevated, limited-access highway on the southern perimeter of downtown, between the city and Lake Ontario. The highway has several on- and off-ramps, feeding from and into the city's grid of streets.

On my way, I watch the taxi meter clicking and counting. Along the expressway stretch, the trip seems economical. I am getting quite a bit of distance for my money. Then I hit a choke point at an exit ramp, and from then on everything changes. The rest of my trip is very expensive. Considering what it is costing me, I am getting very little distance. I am not complaining about this. As research, it is economical. What worries me, rather, is the expensive burden on the city, and the planet, of the air pollution and urban road congestion that the expensive part of my trip is registering.

The driver must weave circuitously around a block, then around another block, and so on, to reach the correct side of the correct block of the correct street on which to deposit me. All the way to my micro-destination, from the moment we enter the street grid from the ramp, we are surrounded by delivery vans, other taxis, and private cars whose drivers are also circuitously attempting to reach *their* micro-destinations. Drivers who must park their cars while they attend a meeting, get a tooth filled, call on a customer, or attend to other downtown business go through an extra crawl to reach a garage or parking spot; so much the worse for them. Our joint circuitous congestion hampers all the others attempting to make use of the streets: public transit vehicles, pedestrians, bicycle couriers.

In vain, I long to leave the taxi and walk directly to my destination. The taxi can travel only indirectly. I mollify myself with the knowledge that my situation informs me of the identical situation of drivers with packages or couriered mail to deliver or cars to stash. Everyone in a vehicle has become a prisoner of the grid and the limited and indirect access to it in this exasperating system. How different it is from the free and convenient downtown grid I experienced when I could walk and could get unlimited access into it at every corner, not merely at arbitrary choke points.

It dawned upon me at length that two separate, major misconceptions were buried in this mess.

Misconception One is expressed in the elevated limited-access highway and its ramps, whose designers should have asked themselves, "How can we help this great diversity of users reach their great diversity of micro-destinations most directly?" Instead, they apparently asked themselves, "How can people reach a macro-destination, downtown, most speedily?"

When my taxi enters the downtown grid from the north or west, which are not furnished with limited-access expressways, my trip within the downtown is so much more economical than when I enter the grid from the expressway at the south that the entire trip is more economical despite my avoidance of the small expressway stretch. How ironic that the ambitious, elevated behemoth of an expressway and its land-wasting ramps are counterproductive for drivers using the downtown. It would be a wonder if closing a road designed to express Misconception One didn't result in at least a 20 percent reduction in vehicular travel without a single vehicle actually vanishing.

Misconception Two is expressed in the NO LEFT TURN, NO STANDING (during busy hours), and ONE WAY, ONE WAY, and ONE WAY signs, the impediments forcing my driver all around Robin Hood's barn to reach a micro-destination. These impediments were contrived to keep vehicles out of one another's way and thus carry out the theme of a speedy trip. What a dreamworld! It would be a wonder if reducing these impediments didn't reduce congestion further after Misconception One's error was eliminated. One American mayor, John Norquist of Milwaukee, has made a start with such an experiment by eliminating one-way streets; he calls his city's popular program friendly driving.

The chief impediment in the double-barreled mess is obviously a cherished paradigm. In effect, somebody told traffic engineers and road designers that *the journey matters more than the destination*—an inappropriate analogy about a philosophical approach to life—and they believed it. In the background of this paradigm I see little boys with toy cars happily murmuring "*Zoom, Zooom, Zooooom!*"

The fact that university students in this so-called discipline are not informed of evidence that has long been available tells us that such evidence is uncongenial to their teachers. The cherished but deformed paradigm is poison that harms everything it touches—damaging community life; wasting time, energy, and land; polluting air; and vitiating the independence of countries with large oil reserves. This is also a "perfect" example of antiscience masquerading as the science it has betrayed: first it went wrong with a fruitless question based on misconception of purpose; a wrong hypothesis followed; next came ignored evidence; when the evidence could no longer be ignored, it was not seen as opening up further questions, and that failure killed off the traffic enterprise as a coherent, expanding body of knowledge.

In the meantime, each year students have poured forth from universities, a clear, harmful case of education surrendered to credentialism. One wonders at the docility of the students who evidently must be satisfied enough with the credentials to be uncaring about the lack of education. The credentials may indeed be a good investment for them but are not a good investment for society. That anxious parent at the forum (p.48) was well advised to worry about change in university education.

The next example demonstrates how even one wrong turning in the scientific state of mind—in this case, the wrong choice of an investigative strategy—can betray science.

Three great scientists in the nineteenth century laid the foundations of all modern public health measures. I have alluded to two of them already in this chapter: Louis Pasteur, a chemist and bacteriologist in Paris; and Dr. John Snow, a physician and pathologist in London, who discovered that cholera infection spread through contaminated drinking water. Snow noticed that the high disease and death rates of a district in central London coincided with a particular water source, the Broad Street pump.

To make sure his hypothesis was solid, Snow tracked down every seeming anomaly (cases turning up elsewhere; an eventual drop in mortality rates) and accounted factually for the connection of each to the Broad Street drinking water, thus rendering order from confusion. His work is a scientific classic, not only for its important discovery but also for his meticulous compiling of evidence. When he presented the evidence to governmental authorities in London, they instantly removed the handle from the Broad Street pump and the epidemic halted. Snow's hypothesis was immediately tested by the real world and validated.

The third of these geniuses was Dr. Edward Jenner, who noticed that English milkmaids who contracted cowpox, a mild disease, escaped the ravages of smallpox. He hypothesized that the mild form of the disease must be a protection against the virulent form. This suggested the idea of a protective vaccine, which not only brought smallpox under control by vaccination but also laid the foundation for many other types of protective vaccines and, eventually, for knowledge of immune systems. Jenner mentally compared individuals who had contracted cowpox with those who had not. All modern statistical methods in which individuals are matched against similar individuals, some of whom are given placebos and others of whom are given whatever substance or treatment is being investigated, are derived from Jenner's brilliant observation of individual differences and his detective work in identifying the salient difference. This is how researchers have identified vitamin-deficiency diseases, and how new medicines are tested on human beings after first being tested on animals. It is how informed conclusions are reached about the value of tests for detecting cancers at early stages of suspect growths.

Both methods—those comparing environments, as Dr. Snow did, and those comparing individuals, as Dr. Jenner did—are valuable research tools when used appropriately. Either is worthless when used inappropriately—the point of my next example of alarming abandonment of a scientific state of mind.

In the summer of 1995, Chicago endured a vicious heat wave, compounded by high humidity and high ozone levels. In the week of July 14–July 20, more than a thousand patients in excess of the usual number for that period were admitted to hospitals because of heatstroke, dehydration, heat exhaustion, kidney failure, or electrolytic imbalances. Heatstroke victims often suffered permanent damage; many others were successfully treated in hospital emergency rooms. Hundreds died before arriving at hospitals.

Deaths in Chicago during the week were 739 in excess of those in a typical hot summer week—too many for the medical examiner's office to handle. A local meat-packer volunteered his fleet of refrigerated trucks in which to store bodies until the overworked staff of the medical examiner and his volunteers could perform autopsies and certify causes of death. But even the truck fleet couldn't keep up with the influx of corpses, which were predominantly those of poor, elderly people.

Overloaded electric-power transformers failed, rendering air conditioners, televisions, radios, and elevators in some districts useless. Elderly residents of high-rises, including high-rent buildings, had to be carried down from their stifling apartments. Doubled use of water, as sweltering children opened street hydrants, led to losses of water pressure, leaving some buildings without water for days.

Immediately before the heat wave began, meteorologists warned residents to use air conditioners, drink plenty of water each day, and seek cool places, indoors or outdoors, in which to relax. The most appalling circumstance was that large numbers of the elderly dead were found in apartments that were infernally hot, with windows covered and doors locked. Sometimes these people had refused help from worried neighbors and failed to seek refuge in air-conditioned stores.

After the heat wave ended, a large research team from the U.S. Centers for Disease Control and Prevention (CDC) moved in, to see what could be discovered to prevent similar disasters in the future. The researchers carefully paired each dead individual with an otherwise similar survivor of the heat wave. The matching survivor was from a randomly chosen location. This swift and Herculean effort by eighty researchers, their supervisors, and the high-powered designers of the study was worthless, because it turned up only what everybody already knew, including the meteorologists who had issued the early warnings. Those who died had run out of water, had no air-conditioning, did not leave their rooms to find cool refuge, and were not successfully checked up on. Indeed, the researchers' findings were worse than useless. Survivors differed in having successfully kept cool. The findings were misleading because they encouraged blaming the victims; after all, they hadn't looked after themselves. *The New England Journal of Medicine* dignified these discoveries by publishing them, with no criticism of the inappropriate methodology.

In contrast, a young sociology graduate student from New York named Eric Klinenberg took a different approach to the question. He was a native of Chicago, and he noticed that some areas of the city had considerably higher death rates than other areas. His thinking was derived from the type of detective work employed by Dr. Snow. He did pair-matching too, but of communities, not individuals. He chose as his pair two districts with similar or identical microclimates and similar proportions of elderly people living alone. The big difference between his two districts, North Lawndale and South Lawndale, was that the heat-wave death rate in North Lawndale was 40 fatalities per 100,000 population, while right next door, in South Lawndale, the death rate was fewer than 4 per 100,000. Klinenberg thought this was a discrepancy worth looking into. His observations, demographic and historical inquiries, and information from interviews with elderly survivors and others in both districts are reported and analyzed in his book, *Heat Wave,* subtitled *A Social Autopsy of Disaster in Chicago.* Unlike the CDC study, it summarizes much that nobody knew about the contrasting behavior of elderly people in the two areas and the everyday, practical reasons for their differing behavior in time of crisis.

In North Lawndale, where the death rate was so high, elderly people were not accustomed to walking in their district because there was almost nothing for them to walk to. It was a commercial and social desert, almost devoid of stores and other gathering places. Old people were thus unacquainted with storekeepers who could welcome them into air-conditioned space. They were afraid, too, to leave their apartments, for fear these would be burglarized while they were out. For the same reason, they feared strangers who came to check on them. In the crisis they were behaving as they always did in this place with no functioning community. That was perhaps Klinenberg's most horrifying discovery.

In South Lawndale, where a much higher proportion of the elderly survived, everything was diametrically different. There the elderly were accustomed to walking outside. There were plenty of places for them to go on the district's bustling, crowded streets. They knew storekeepers and had no hesitation about hanging around in their air-conditioned spaces, where they also had access to water. They felt secure about leaving their apartments, and they trusted those who came to check on them, some of whom they knew as acquaintances. In the crisis they were behaving much as they always did in this place with a lively, functioning community.

Klinenberg searched beneath the surface, to find the historical reasons for these diametric differences. Everything traced back to extreme differences in density of population in the two districts. North Lawndale had lost most of its former residents to the suburbs, and they had not been replaced by immigrants. Its former industries had rapidly relocated elsewhere or had closed down. The district was full of vacant lots. The population was too thin to support commerce, and therefore was sensibly shunned by newcomers to the city. In contrast, South Lawndale had remained densely enough occupied to stay busy and to attract newcomers—so many newcomers that housing was in short supply, a disadvantage that was minor compared with the emptiness of North Lawndale.

Klinenberg also turned up many interesting nuances about the city's disaster planning. For instance, its organizations of social workers had been stripped of personnel in the interests of saving money, with the idea that police and firemen could take on social workers' tasks in case of emergency. The city assumed that police and firemen had been trained in such tasks because disaster planners had ordered it done. This was an exercise in what is called reinventing government, making governments behave like profit-conscious businesses. The training of police and firemen to behave like social workers didn't take because, Klinenberg noticed, all along the line, from supervisors and chiefs down to new rookies, social work conflicted too much with the police and firemen's profoundly macho ethos.

It is not reassuring to know that the U.S. federal agency entrusted with so vital a responsibility as disease control is so insensitive about the question it asked itself in Chicago and the inappropriate strategy it chose for its research. But I have not told this tale simply to upbraid the CDC for its stupidity in this case, or even to show how much more fruitful one researcher can be than eighty when that one has not made up his mind in advance about what he expects to find and the eighty—with their questionnaires about air-conditioning and refuge-seeking and going outdoors—have.

I am interested in those eighty researchers and what they were thinking. I believe it is important to find this out. I am reminded of the members of the board of directors of Enron, the disgraced energy-trading company that collapsed after a carnival of accounting frauds. When directors were questioned by Congress about their acquiescence in these shenanigans, some said they had individually had their doubts but had suppressed them, to avoid being at odds with their colleagues.

Now, as to those eighty researchers. Among any eighty knowledgeable Americans, at least a few are likely to be skeptical and intelligent, often very much so. That is my experience of Americans, which has been considerable. I think the fruitful question to be asked here is why all eighty behaved as if they had a pressing mission to learn whether air conditioners and water are good for combating heat. Were they so wedded to the statistical method derived from Dr. Jenner's detective work with smallpox that they were ignorant of the history of Dr. Snow's work on environmental health hazards? Did they know how to identify a dangerous environment? A fatal environment? Were any of them potential Klinenbergs, so to speak? If so, why didn't they object to the inappropriate investigative strategy? What would have happened if they did? Would their intelligent input have been respected? Or would they have been regarded as pariahs and troublemakers? What did they themselves think would happen? Had their supervisors been selected because of impressive credentials? Or for knowledge, wisdom, and courage? These things go to the heart of the abandonment of science and the scientific state of mind—a catastrophe we simply can't let happen if it can be stemmed and reversed.

Were these people awed at being part of the exalted CDC? Did they do their work cynically? We had better find out what went wrong, whatever it may be. It is not far-fetched to speculate that our own lives may depend on the intelligence and courage of these people or people like them—and, more important, that the ability of our culture to survive may depend on them or people like them.

Are the great gifts to our culture by Jenner, Snow, and other scientific geniuses to be frittered away? The culture does have people like Klinenberg. Surely he is not really alone (I hope). What he discovered may not be heeded or acted upon. It probably won't be. He himself recognized that effective change would cost money and time, with nothing to show off before the next election. But at least he spoke up with fresh truths drawn from the real world, and that is a beginning. If that is lost, all is lost.

My third and final example of abandonment of the scientific state of mind involves the mysterious materializing of jobs, which has the esthetic merit of symmetry with the mysterious vanishing of traffic; otherwise, the two mysteries bear no relationship to each other except that both are met with obstinate refusal to examine the evidence—in the case of the job mystery, refusal by incurious economists.

During the year 2002, the economic entity called the Greater Toronto Area (GTA)—nicknamed the Golden Horseshoe—has enjoyed a boom that economists said at first couldn't be happening and then "shouldn't" be happening. But it did happen. The reason that it "shouldn't" have been happening is that Canada's economic growth is supposedly led by exports; the United States takes 85 percent of Canada's exports, and the United States was in a recession, and so exports from Canada were down. Canada's economy is indeed heavily dependent on export sales to the United States, but that isn't the entire economic picture.

The first official tidings of the anomaly arrived in April, when Statistics Canada revealed that the country had acquired more than 200,000 net additional jobs during the first quarter of the year, while America had acquired none. By June, the financial papers were daring to write of a roaring economy, "significantly outperforming our major trading partner." In July, with news that "Canada" had added a "stunning 66,400 [more net] jobs" in June while the United States had suffered a net loss of 150,000 nonfarm jobs so far during the year, eminent economists consulted by the media could offer no explanations. But at least they were admitting, finally, that it was happening. "Six months ago when Statistics Canada released its January employment report, the [economic] forecasting community wondered whether the numbers were somehow incorrect," a financial columnist reported. "But now, with six months of data, economists are no longer doubters. . . . It's for real."

The reason I've put "Canada" in quotation marks in the paragraph above is that a large part of the country is economically stagnant or declining, and to understand what is going on behind national statistics on jobs, one must know where the jobs are being added or lost. It never happens amorphously, in the country as a whole. Everything that happens in the world happens at some place.

My guess was that the jobs were being added specifically in the GTA and that they were materializing because the area was experiencing a significant episode of city import replacing, a process in which companies typically begin providing bits and pieces of producers' goods and services that were formerly imported. This process is led neither by export sales nor by sales to consumers. It is led only by perceived opportunity. Since such jobs don't fit into economists' preconceptions of how economies behave, they don't recognize these jobs as respectable evidence of economic expansion, and thus fail to recognize the process.

A number of clues suggested city import replacing. First were bits of anecdotal evidence from manufacturers in the

Toronto area that, yes, they were purchasing locally various items that they formerly had to import; second, the Canadian dollar was gently rising in value, which is exactly what happens during significant city import replacing. And third, Statistics Canada, in an unrelated release, reported that Vaughan was currently the fastest growing "city" in Canada.

And I know personally of a machine maker in another small GTA town that has been bought as a subsidiary by a large factory in Mississauga, also in the GTA, specifically to supply needs which that factory formerly met through imports.

Woodbridge is a suburb directly across the street from Toronto, at the northernmost border of the city. It is a subdivision of a larger suburb named Vaughan, which in turn is a political subdivision of a suburban and exurban sprawl called York. Vaughan has many gated, expensive housing tracts, along with the usual suburban complement of shopping malls. Except for a tiny heart of shops around a public square along with a large apartment house, at the center of Woodbridge, where one actually sees human beings walking, there is nothing physically resembling a city. But the heart, including the apartment building and a scattering of old houses left over from the time when this was a country town, is humanly scaled, pleasant, and physically welcoming. Two of my neighbors and I decided to drive up to Vaughan on a beautiful autumn Saturday and see what changes had been going on there.

The big changes were Vaughan's huge new suburban factory parks, each filled with dozens of new, and mostly handsome, buildings, rather small as factories go, each announcing its specialty, such as tool and die making or injection molding. Most impressive were the clusters of new factories, cheek by jowl, that were providing construction components. Some clusters were formed by companies specializing in various metal or glass components, or items combining those two materials. Other clusters, in different factory parks, were devoted to all manner of construction components in wood. Still another, smaller cluster featured textiles.

Neither I nor my two companions are personally equipped to gather the important economic information that an episode of city import replacing merits—such as what items were those with which the episode started; what was the previous history of companies engaged in the process; what new departures have been most and least successful; what are the advantages to customers who formerly imported the items: Lower cost? Time savings? Convenience? Closer adherence to desired specifications? If not these, then what? Where did the necessary capital come from? Had any of the new companies yet begun to export, as well as to supply GTA enterprises? And where did the workers holding these new manufacturing jobs live? (Obviously not in the mansions in the new gated housing tracts.) It being a Saturday, since the three of us work weekdays too, the new factories were closed and we didn't encounter anyone in the factory parks, nor did we speak with anyone else, with one exception that I will mention later. This is a thoroughly car-dependent suburb, the kind of place where one must drive and park to pick up a loaf of bread or a bottle of vanilla. But at least we could see what was plainly in front of our eyes.

The second fastest-growing city in Canada at present is Brampton, which is larger and older than Vaughan, but is also a suburb in the Greater Toronto Area. It ranks behind Vaughan in growth only because Statistics Canada likes putting these matters in percentages and Brampton has been growing from a much larger base than Vaughan.* In absolute terms, Brampton's growth is the greater. From May 2001 to December 2002, Brampton's population increased by 27,000, reaching 352,000. Its net jobs increased by 3,500 in 2001 and another 3,500 in 2002, on top of a 4,000 increase in 2000. In 2002 it was second in Canada only to the City of Toronto in value of building permits issued. While Brampton is a suburb, it is not a bedroom community. It has an unusually large, attractive, and urban core, employing more than five thousand people in shops and services mainly originated in Brampton, not as chain stores or franchises. Its new residents, as for many years past, include large contingents from India and from the poor regions of Canada, especially Newfoundland, followed (in this order) by smaller contingents from Britain, Portugal, Guyana, Italy, the Philippines, Trinidad and Tobago, Pakistan, and Poland. The population includes 40 percent (about 141,000 individuals) classified by Statistics Canada as "visible minorities," predominantly from South Asia. Brampton makes a deliberate effort to retain its immigrants, attaching them firmly to the community by its quality of life, its schools, and its opportunities in the arts, professions, entrepreneurship, and employment. About half of Brampton's job-holding residents work in Brampton, another quarter in nearby suburbs (including Vaughan); the other quarter

---

*Such percentages are ill-conceived for useful information. A hamlet that grows from six people to twelve and adds one new job to a former single job would be the fastest-growing place in both population and jobs in a given year, unless another hamlet exceeded 100 percent. And if a household in such a hamlet added a porch, that could register as an impressive percentage gain in building permits.

commute to the City of Toronto. Brampton has one of the lowest crime rates in Canada, and it may be one of the country's most cosmopolitan and economically sophisticated communities.

Most Brampton jobs are in manufacturing (of all kinds, ranging from low-tech food processing, bottling, and automobile assembly to high-tech robotics, pharmaceutical chemistry, and engineering of automotive engine parts). Most jobs are in the hundreds of acres of industrial parks located between the Toronto international airport to the south and residential and downtown Brampton to the north. So much is occurring simultaneously in Brampton's vast manufacturing economy—expansion of some companies, contraction of others, new exporting work, new investment, and so on—that the trees threaten to get lost in the woods.

However, when I asked Dennis Cutajar, director of the Brampton business development department, about import-replacement jobs specifically, he pointed out that most factories in the industrial parks now include offices that front on the industrial parks' main roads. Formerly these factories were devoted exclusively to manufacturing and its industrial ancillary facilities, such as transportation, warehousing, and storage. But beginning in the 1980s, he said, a new trend has emerged: executives are now locating their headquarters as close as possible to the factory floor, the space where production takes place. With the executives come other jobs: in administration, research, engineering, design, and marketing, very good jobs, using high levels of skill. These changes in corporate organization give Brampton services that were formerly located in downtowns elsewhere and imported into Brampton. He estimates that about ten thousand of Brampton's net new jobs are corporate headquarters jobs, many located in former factory buildings. One begins to understand why Brampton (Vaughan, too) lacks suburban office parks and clusters of downtown office towers. One also begins to understand why high vacancy rates have persisted in recently built office towers in downtown Toronto in spite of rent reductions, and why some older office buildings there and in other large cities have become available for such uses as condominiums and live-work spaces for self-employed people. The tenants that made possible the imposing skyscraper landscapes of the world's downtowns have begun finding other landscapes to populate. Mr. Cutajar says he now observes the trend is affecting financial offices, as executives move corporate headquarters of banks, for example, to what used to be their cheap, outlying back offices for check clearing and other routine production activities. Cost reductions for space, he said, have apparently become more attractive than the geographical proximity of bank headquarters to one another and to the corporate law firms and the national or multinational firms with which they transact business—which have already, themselves, dispersed out of the towering downtowns of the old economy. To help prepare its population for the ingenuity and knowledge economy, Brampton has helped finance a campus of Sheridan College Institute of Technology and Advanced Learning to educate workers in manufacturing skills. Many workers in the new corporate offices learned their skills in computer-aided design or graphics, or as science technicians and administrators, at Sheridan.

When headquarters jobs shift from downtown Toronto to Brampton, the movement is not import replacement because the metropolitan area involved is one economic entity. But when they shift from distant cities or other countries, as also happens, it is import replacement.

Cheaper space doesn't mean Spartan space. The offices converted from former factory buildings can be stunning. The one I examined was that of Nortel, where a friend of mine from Sri Lanka who works there showed me around. Nortel is a Canadian-originated multinational corporation that makes cables and switching equipment for the Internet and other communications systems. The architects—a New York firm—who converted some of Nortel's factory buildings to headquarters offices made imaginative use of the factory skylights and the opportunities they gave for placing small gardens, highlighting artworks, and giving character and identity to functionally different sorts of spaces (lounges, conference rooms, workstations, and corridors). Progressing through the large floor, one also catches glimpses of external vistas at ground level. At Nortel these include fountains and ponds where Canada geese are raising goslings. Office space in towers is ascetic, even though more expensive, in comparison with what can be wrought from former factory buildings.

At Nortel, the most expensive, state-of-the-art office chairs are those designed by Herman Miller in New York, which are advertised in *The New Yorker*. I was struck also by the more modest but sturdy, comfortable, and elegant painted wood-compound and steel-rod chairs in the big dining area, to which office workers bring take-out food and home-packed lunches. They were unlike usual furniture. Turning a chair upside down for a clue to its provenance, I found a label reporting "Made in Canada"; probably more import replacing. I can imagine these chairs becoming favorites among upscale consumers, for dining and side chairs. When I mentioned this to Mr. Cutajar, he said that a recent analysis he has made of Brampton products shows that furniture has become one of the five product categories most rapidly growing in value. A prowl among offices in industrial parks might suggest further grist for import replacing and innovation.

The most conspicuous building in all of Brampton is a little Victorian bandshell more than a century old, in Gage Park at the heart of downtown. When the parkland was given to Brampton at the turn of the twentieth century, the deed stipulated that if the bandshell were ever demolished, the land must revert to the Gage family estate. There the beautifully maintained, jewellike bandstand sits, the frivolous guardian of a lovely and intact park on the most valuable real estate in Brampton. It is encircled by a summer promenade that in the long winters becomes a winding public rink for pleasure skating. The bandshell insists loudly, but with good humor, that Brampton is unique, has its own character, its own history, and is humane. True, but all is not sweetness and enlightenment in Brampton.

The place has a huge problem: *traffic.* The mayor, Susan Fennell, is aware that traffic must be greatly alleviated, and soon, and that more roads and interchanges are not the answer. She makes the point repeatedly and publicly that people must get out of their private cars and into public transit vehicles; she is aware that to make this happen, public transit must provide faster service, extended hours, extended routes, and low fares. Brampton Transit works hard to deliver, plowing earnings back into those aims, but the slow progress makes painful reading: "Route 3, midday service improved from every 60 minutes to every 30 minutes . . . Evening trips extended by two, operating till 8 p.m. . . . route 15, the 40-minute midday frequency is changed to a 30-minute frequency. . . . Route 50, a new route, operates on a 60-minute frequency during AM and PM rush hours, Monday through Friday. . . ." But angry town meetings on the horrors of traffic congestion do not address the point that the mayor makes; or, at any rate, the newspapers' reports of the meetings say only what they have been reporting for many decades—that the public demands more and wider roads. The reports may be true, more's the pity.

To me, the most astonishing aspect of this economic expansion is the continued inability of Canadian economists to credit what is right in front of their eyes if they would only look. As the months of 2002 rolled on, with headlines about Canada's mysterious "job creation machine" and an economy that "beats analysts' expectations," the economists consulted by the media—people like the chief economist and assistant chief economist of the Royal Bank of Canada, the senior economist and senior capital markets strategist of the Toronto-Dominion Bank, the chief economist of J. P. Morgan Securities Canada, the currency strategist of Citigroup, New York, and the chief economist of Merrill Lynch Canada—expressed a consensus that the phenomenon must be "consumer led" by people's additional demands for houses and cars. To be sure, as always happens when desirable new jobs are plentiful, people were buying more houses and cars, just as they were buying more orange juice and shoes. This is a "multiplier effect," long familiar in economics, but to cite it does not explain how consumers have earned sufficiently more money to exert this effect. Economists understand this. Yet, when compelled to abandon, reluctantly, their standard babble about export-led economic life, they sought refuge in a consumer-led explanation which they themselves must have been aware was hollow, both theoretically and in view of the evidence itself, had they looked at the evidence, which apparently they did not. Certainly, consumers can enrich themselves by borrowing on inflated house values, and they had been doing so (see p. 31), but U.S. homeowners have been taking even greater advantage of these windfalls than Canadians, so some additional expansion process has had to be operating in Canada.

For the first half of the year 2002, Canada added 460,000 net new jobs, while in the same period the United States added only 5,000, with an economy ten times the size of Canada's. When August figures came out in November, economists became more comfortable than they had been. Although August's was the eleventh consecutive monthly job gain, the expansion was small compared with July's, and many of the new jobs were part-time. Confident forecasts emphasized that economic sectors such as mining, logging, and agriculture, important contributors to the country's export trade, were declining, and forecasters looked forward to the unseemly economic behavior winding down and ending. Alas for them. When figures for November came out, in December, they showed a gain of 55,300 net new jobs. "Economists found the strength of yesterday's report particularly shocking," wrote a business reporter,

> because Canada's job market had slowed in September and October as employment gains downshifted to part-time positions at the expense of full-time. That trend reversed in November . . . more than offsetting the drop in full-time employment in the two prior months. "The labor market looked like it was getting a bit tired, but it sure

woke up again in November," said . . . [the] chief economist at the Royal Bank of Canada. "Canada's numbers are
particularly 'eye-popping' when compared with the United
States which yesterday reported it lost a further 40,000 jobs
in November," [he] added. . . . "What can I say?" said
[the] senior economist at [the investment firm] BMO
Nesbitt Burns. "It's nothing short of remarkable."

Probably it will be forgotten, lost to memory, like the
episode of city import replacing that occurred in the early
1990s in Vancouver at a time when the rest of Canada, including Toronto, was in recession. The Vancouver event slid
by without being identified or studied, it seems. As for the
general public, it gets about as much enlightenment from all
the professors of economics it supports as from the professors
of traffic engineering.

It will be unfortunate if this episode in the Greater Toronto Area sinks into oblivion. Here is a marvelous opportunity for economics teachers and their students to study a
significantly large, living, breathing event in the very process
of carrying on and, in due course, winding down. Perhaps we
would learn why these episodes happen in so few Canadian
cities.

One of the besetting sins of Americans is that they don't
seem to think that any place outside the United States is totally real; their curiosity about Canada seems almost nonexistent. But American economists, too, ought to be interested
in this Canadian episode of import replacing, which may
help explain some of the jobs lost in the United States. More
important, they might learn why these episodes have become
so infrequent in American cities, where they were once very
common. I have some ideas on that, too (see Notes, p. 198);

however, reasoned but undisciplined guesses are no substitute for the rigors of genuine scientific inquiry.

The combination of the appearance of professional respect for scientific rigor coupled with professional contempt for scientifically rigorous behavior is toxic, a poison that infects more activities in North America than the few I have pointed out here. It cripples foreign aid programs, pedagogy, and illegal-drug policies, and it promotes dubious and harmful medical treatment fads, nutrition and other lifestyle advice, and agricultural recommendations.

Science has also been making little progress in dealing with whole systems; particularly in biology and medical treatment, it tends to become arrested in the stage of singling out isolated bits, with little grasp of how these interact with other bits of integrated systems. Very partial understanding combined with typical scientific overconfidence emboldens us to accept mistakes we would not otherwise accept.

Our culture has survived much bad science in the past, such as phrenology and claims that men with dark skins, and women of any hue, lack the intellectual capabilities of white men. Why can't we continue surviving bad science? To people who didn't venture more than a dozen miles from home, it didn't matter whether the world was round or flat. Bad farming practices in the past resulted in poor yields and depleted soils; today chemical fertilizers, toxic sprays, and doses of hormones and antibiotics to livestock endanger not only soils but also the health of farmers, farm laborers, consumers, and the environment. Modern life has raised the ante of knowledge required in everything from science to democratic participation. Failures were always stultifying; now they can be devastating.

If the rot of bad science continues to spread, to be tolerated, and even to be rewarded by corporations and centrally administered government grants, the heyday of scientific and technological achievement is inevitably drawing to its end in North America. Try to imagine how demoralizing that deterioration will be for a culture that almost worships science, and that proudly connects its identity and prowess with scientific and technological superiority. How will such a culture and its people deal with becoming incompetent and backward in science and science-based technology?

A postscript about Vaughan, Brampton, and food: my companions and I spend quite a lot of time eating on our exploratory forays into the fringes of the Greater Toronto Area. This always yields surprises. In Vaughan we happened upon a lovely place selling delicious Italian ice cream in more than fifty flavors. The secret of its excellence is that the proprietor always makes the gelato fresh—all those flavors!—the night before he puts it on sale, and no flavor is artificial. He told us he had come from Sicily a few years previously, and first established his store and kitchen in North York, an undistinguished City of Toronto suburb adjoining Vaughan. There the enterprise failed. One of my companions—the author of guidebooks to economical Toronto restaurants—gave the proprietor well-informed suggestions of where, in the city proper, the establishment would be likely to succeed. The suggestions were appreciated by the proprietor, who made notes because, he said, he and his backers were interested in either franchising or establishing a second outlet. Thus can strangers in a city casually help one another. This gelato maker is a fortunate and sensible man. He has pride in his product and a flair for enjoying his customers and his life. Each year, he told us, he removes the chairs and tables from his outdoor patio in December, and by Christmas closes the shop and departs for Florida until March, when he reopens for business. Here's a genuine consumer economic activity, but even so, it lives on the multiplier effect of economic expansion from other causes, which also supports its proprietor's annual three-month sojourn in Florida.

In Brampton, we were charmed and well fed in a downtown restaurant calling itself a 1950s diner. It is more handsomely designed and spacious than a diner, but its menu includes authentic 1950s diner items, such as potato soup; Reuben, western, and clubhouse sandwiches on white toast; and root beer ice-cream sodas. The diner also appeals to nostalgic interest in car and truck design of the 1950s. The banquette where I sat was flanked by the unbelievably vulgar and cumbersome fender of a pink Cadillac. A display case contains model cars and trucks of that bygone time. A miniature McDonald's truck is innocent of golden arches; instead, it is emblazoned with the fifteen-cent price of its hamburgers. A tall cylindrical case with a revolving interior contains pies with the highest, fluffiest meringues I have ever seen. In this diner, clearly you wander into somebody's dream. The only way to enjoy it is to go to Brampton and enjoy the rest of the downtown too.

CHAPTER FIVE

Dumbed-Down Taxes

Henri Pirenne tells us that the low point of the Dark Age that followed Western Rome's collapse occurred about the year 1000. After that, instead of sinking ever deeper into incompetent poverty, our ancestral culture slowly took a turn for the better. Pirenne also analyzes why and how culture's trajectory pivoted upward. The poor, backward European cities—many of them, at the time, hardly more than embryos of cities, with Venice leading the way and others following—began trading with one another again and, indirectly through Venice, with the Middle East and Asia. The cities developed by importing, creating, and exporting innovations. By trading and mutually adopting innovations, they slowly drew abreast of advanced Asian cities and then surpassed them in economic and social capability and prosperity.

Disadvantaged in almost every way though they were, the early medieval cities typically benefited from *subsidiarity* and *fiscal accountability*.

Subsidiarity is the principle that government works best—most responsibly and responsively—when it is closest to the people it serves and the needs it addresses. *Fiscal accountability* is the principle that institutions collecting and disbursing taxes work most responsibly when they are transparent to those providing the money.

The cities of the Roman Empire had lost these advantages in the desperate years before the collapse, when the imperial treasury extorted from them as much as it could and disbursed the money for schemes and needs according to its own, frequently crazed, priorities. The early medieval cities regained the two principles slowly, in various ways. Some, like London, received royal charters authorizing them to farm (that is, collect) their own taxes. Others, like Hamburg and cities of the Low Countries and northern France, gained subsidiarity and fiscal accountability through the efforts of merchants and citizens united by common interests and then, increasingly, by custom. Many others, like Venice itself, Florence, Bologna, and Genoa, achieved subsidiarity and fiscal accountability as by-products of their own sovereignty as city-states.

Both principles are important, but the need for subsidiarity has become especially acute, for reasons I shall sketch out later. Yet both subsidiarity and fiscal accountability of public money have almost disappeared from the modern world, as if a cycle is returning to the Roman imperium, rather than to principles that renewed Western culture long after Rome's failure. Today, over almost all the world, major taxes, including those most remunerative and most economically informative, like income taxes based on ability to pay, or those directly reflecting economic expansion, like sales or value-added taxes, are collected either by sovereign governments or by their surrogates, provincial governments. This is true of federal governments like those of the United States, Canada, Mexico, and Germany, and of centralized sovereignties like those of England, France, Sweden, and Israel—to name a few of both types. The only exceptions are a few city-states like Hong Kong and Singapore and near-city-states like the Czech Republic (the city-state of Prague), Slovakia (the city-state of Bratislava), and Taiwan (the city-state of Taipei). Only very minor taxation, such as property taxes, responsive neither to ability to pay nor to economic expansion, is typically permitted to cities.

Because city sources of public revenue are frequently inadequate to needs, so-called senior governments sporadically come to their aid with grants of public money and programs devised for using the grants. These resources are disbursed into many different localities, currently in many different situations, with unlike needs and dissimilar opportunities. Sovereign governments cannot possibly be in intimate touch with all this variation. Even with the best will in the world, the disbursers must act as if common denominators exist, and if these cannot be found, will allow idiosyncratic needs and opportunities to go unanswered. An example is a stillborn hotel tax in Toronto. The numbers of tourists visiting the city have declined since the late 1990s. The city has had virtually no money for marketing itself or its events as tourist destinations, so hotels in the city asked the City Council to tax hotel rooms modestly to raise such funds. When the city government boldly passed the requested tax, the provincial government annulled the act; only the province could enact such a tax, and only by making it a province-wide policy. Other hotels in the province, most notably in Windsor, a virtual suburb of Detroit across the river, vigorously resisted the tax, in the case of Windsor on the reasonable grounds that it wouldn't help that city's economy.

The social and economic needs of urban residents and businesses are extremely varied and complex compared with those of simpler settlements. They require wide ranges of awareness and knowledge that are humanly beyond the comprehension of functionaries in distant institutions, who try to overcome that handicap by devising programs that disregard particulars on the assumption that one size can fit all, which is untrue. Even when sovereignties and provinces or states give special grants to this or that locality, the special grants almost always reflect the priorities of the disbursing institutions, not those of the recipient settlements.

So dysfunctional have these ordinary arrangements become that in North America associations of mayors of municipalities, and associations of municipalities themselves, have taken to expressing their disappointments and dissatisfactions loudly, sometimes at screaming levels. The Organization for Economic Cooperation and Development (OECD), composed of thirty currently rich countries, published a report in 2002, *Cities for Citizens: Improving Metropolitan Governance,* the purport of which is that something is wrong which needs fixing.

The disconnection between public treasuries and local domestic needs drawing upon them does not exist within taxpayers' pockets or bank accounts. The same taxpayers supply money for all layers of government. Rather, the disconnection is purely administrative and governmental. It is a political artifact with the strength of bureaucratic tradition. That being so, the dumbed-down result should theoretically be simple to mend; but, if experience in Canada is a guide, it can't be mended. If it were only true that necessity is the mother of invention, we would have here a political invention on the verge of happening, but since *opportunity* is actually the mother of invention, this needed political invention hasn't materialized. The closest things to such events happening in our times are the peaceful separation of Singapore from Malaysia, and the peaceful separation of Czechoslovakia into the two sovereignties of the Czech Republic and Slovakia. But in most countries such separation would risk terrorism and warfare, as has happened in Sri Lanka, Cyprus, and Chechnya and has been threatened elsewhere in places too numerous to mention. Besides, nothing stands still; even successful and peaceful acts of separation that confer subsidiarity and fiscal responsibility because of sovereignties' smallness do not answer the question of what will happen when those sovereignties grow out of touch with newly growing localities and their needs, perhaps with influxes of immigrant populations.

Dumbed-down use of taxes—and the dumbed-down use of powers the taxes make possible—imposes deterioration, and it is surprising how rapidly this can happen once it gets under way. Toronto used pleasantly to surprise visitors and travel writers by its combination of civilized urban grooming and civil manners with exuberantly cosmopolitan diversity of population, activities, and street scenes. It was not only a rewarding place to visit, no matter what the weather, but a fine place to live. Peter Ustinov flatteringly described Toronto as "New York run by the Swiss."

No longer does the description ring wittily true. Toronto's former neatness and cleanliness have so much degenerated that a visitor (me) to Richmond, Virginia, and San Francisco now enviously notices how clean, in comparison with Toronto, those cities are. The Toronto workers who used to sweep up street litter after garbage and recycling trucks had passed through, and pick up in parks after busy weekends, have vanished for lack of money to pay them. Homeless, ragged panhandlers pop forth belligerently or pathetically from semi-sheltering doorsteps. They bed down atop subway grilles and under park benches and tables. They also crowd to overflowing church basements and other dormitory shelters where, according to public health workers, antibiotic-resistant tuberculosis is spreading. Torontonians returning from summers or sabbaticals away cite litter and homelessness when they speak of culture shock on their return.

They also mention noticing a disquieting surliness or public sullenness: impatience, impoliteness, rage. These are more subtle signs that Toronto has become a city in crisis, indeed in multiple crises.

The formerly excellent public transit system is starved for operating funds. Any grants it has received for many years from the federal or provincial governments have been for capital expenditures on a very few lines, which only increased operating expenses, and which have been so ill-chosen as routes (more about that later) that they are not lucrative. The local transit authority thus lacks money to maintain and repair equipment, or to respond intelligently to increases in city population and employment. To try to make do, it trims service and raises fares. Subways, streetcars, and feeder buses have become intolerably overcrowded in rush hours; for the first time in its history, the system is experiencing serious declines in ridership during a period of rising employment (and thus of rising need for public transit). It is caught in the vicious spiral of poorer service, declining patronage, and rising fares.

As transit riders decrease, pollution indices from car emissions increase. The summer of 2002 generated unprecedented numbers of days—eighteen—with smog sufficiently evil for health officials to warn vulnerable citizens to close their windows and stay indoors. Hospitals receive unprecedented numbers of children with asthma, which has become the single largest reason for admission of children to hospitals. Not surprisingly, the highest smog levels are in excessively car-dependent suburbs, most notably in Oshawa, east of Toronto, the General Motors company town of Canada.

Between 1996 and 2002, Toronto suffered a net loss of 17,515 rental housing units, mostly to developers who can make bigger profits by building and marketing condominiums. Only the few richest households can afford the many fewer apartments or houses for rent, particularly those built before the Second World War, which theoretically should be trickling down to the poor, but which are desirable and costly after renovation and are located in the most lively and interesting neighborhoods. Against the massive losses of rental units, only seventy-four (yes, 74) subsidized apartments affordable by low-wage earners, single-income families, disabled persons, and others on welfare have been added to the city's housing stock in more than a decade. Building this pittance required nine years of strenuous and devoted effort on the part of a band of community volunteers; among many barriers they surmounted was a development tax of more than $1,200 per apartment, extorted to anticipate public schooling costs of tenants' children.

In Chapter 2 I mentioned that assisted-housing policies, designs, and management had become unpopular with both tenants and taxpayers and, like public housing in the United

States, had been drastically curtailed in Canada. However, owing to the good fortune of a clever, courageous, and popular mayor, David Crombie; a housing commissioner, Michael Dennis, who was a genius at cutting red tape; creative architects; and strong citizen support, Toronto managed to win independence from the province for planning and design of assisted housing in 1972. It also extricated itself from the federal government's red tape.

The city used its new responsibilities to build on very small, scattered sites. Architecturally the buildings varied, depending on existing surroundings; on streets with grand old Victorian houses, the infilled assisted housing sported cone-topped turrets and bay windows. Dreary vacant lots were knit back into lively city fabric. The new policies were economical because small sites were unattractive to competing developers with deep pockets; yet small sites added up as they were built upon by cooperatives, public bodies, and other nonprofit builders. No longer was new assisted housing set apart from the normal city, nor its residents stigmatized as project dwellers. If their incomes rose, they tended to stay by choice, making it feasible to raise rents when tenants' incomes rose, which released money to augment further infilling.

For twenty years, Toronto built assisted housing in this fashion, incorporating many constructive innovations in addition to the few I've mentioned. The program was popular with both taxpayers and residents, yet it was felled by one-size-fits-all bureaucracy. When the federal and provincial governments halted grants for assisted housing, Toronto's resources for it were cut off, too. Instead of learning from innovations and encouraging them to spread, the senior governments killed them. Death to innovation is death to economic and so-cial development.

When I go to our neighborhood shopping street, I am asked by a well-spoken, shabbily dressed man of late middle age to write that he and others in his fix need rooming houses, but rooming houses are gone. "Please tell it, spread the word," he says. I promise I will; he thanks me, and I don't have the heart to tell him that spreading the word does no good.

Here comes fiscal accountability: by agreement, the sover-eign federal government and the provinces are supposed to share costs for the health and hospital system. But a curious thing happens. When the federal government grants addi-tional funds to the province to be disbursed for that purpose, our province, along with some others, has been deducting an equivalent amount from their own contributions, raised from their own taxes. Neither the federal government nor citizens have been able to learn what provincial kleptocracies do with these windfalls. Similar sleight of hand occurs with federal grants to provinces for licensed day care for preschool chil-dren; in this case, however, the province chooses to spend the money not for licensed day care but for grants to families in which mothers do not work—because the neoconservatives running the province object ideologically to working moth-ers. (Before that government was elected, it promised to sup-port expanded day care. So did the federal government.) Lack of fiscal accountability leaves cities, which need the day care, and the federal government, which allocates some money for it, both helpless to achieve the expansion.

Apart from attacks on the health system, the debasements that have caused the angriest mass protests, and probably the most anxiety to parents, have been economies stripping the once-excellent Toronto public school system. In a city and region that receives half the foreign immigrants of the entire country, speaking more than eighty mother tongues, teachers of English as a second language have been all but eliminated, and school libraries have been stripped of librarians. Music and other arts programs have been deleted as extravagant frills, a contempt also visited on all manner of Toronto artists and groups such as theater and dance companies, for whom small grants previously received from the city made the difference between a frugal existence and no existence.

The greatest stress on parents and children, judging by protests, has been aroused by school closings—dozens of them, with more continually threatened. Most of these were genuine neighborhood schools to which children could walk or bicycle. They were also accessible to handicapped children, for many of whom special programs and teachers—also chipped away—had made normal schooling possible. Once, schools were relied on as community centers, but youth groups and other volunteer community service groups are now charged so heavily for classroom use for meetings, and for gyms, cafeterias, and auditoriums for other activities, that groups like the Girl Guides and Boy Scouts can't afford the fees. Community use of schools dropped 43 percent between 2000 and 2002. In 2003, 350 after-school courses, ranging from piano and art lessons to computers and graphic design, were cut: no more "lifelong learning" for retired people, immigrants, and other citizens. New fees were added even for groups using outdoor basketball courts and baseball fields. Schools built when taxpayers and parents were still permitted to take pride in them have been disproportionately doomed because their generous corridors and handsome lobbies exceed mean-spirited formulas for allowable square meters of building space per student. By such measures, a culture's social capital is systematically squandered.

Toronto's desperate cheeseparing is not driven by economic necessity. As explained in the previous chapter, it happened to coincide, in 2002, with an unusual economic expansion in the metropolitan area. Nor does it reflect stinginess on the part of taxpayers. According to the Board of Trade, composed of city businesses, in 2001 the federal government collected $20 billion from Toronto taxpayers in income, sales, and excise taxes, of which an indeterminate but lesser amount was returned to the locality in the form of government expenditures for goods and services, payments to consultants and other contractors supplying goods and services to the sovereign government, interest payments to pension funds and other holders of government bonds, transfer payments to individuals qualifying under national programs, and special grants. Federal budget figures are lumped into Canada-wide expenditures, making it impossible to learn how much goes to specific localities and for what purposes. The chairman of the federal parliamentary caucus for Toronto and its region claims he has been unable to identify billions that supposedly have gone annually to the Greater Toronto Area. Even a member of the prime minister's own parliamentary task force, assigned to study and report on municipal needs and problems, says the task force was also left in the dark. So much, once again, for fiscal accountability. "How can you measure the effectiveness of existing programs or propose new ones," he asked, "if you can't get that kind of information?"

Research by Glen Murray, the mayor of Winnipeg—the poorest of Canada's half-dozen large cities (Toronto is the richest)—estimates that Winnipeg residents and businesses pay annually about $7 billion in federal, provincial, and municipal taxes. "But only six percent of that finds its way into municipal coffers." He estimates Toronto's contribution to federal, provincial, and municipal taxes in 2001 was $21 billion. Estimates of the proportion of the total going to the city treasury ranged between 4.5 percent and 6 percent, because the city had to depend so largely on yields from its residential property taxes.

Canadian taxpayers recognize and accept that federal income, sales, and excise taxes must cover the normal costs of a sovereign government. They recognize, too, that a high proportion of Toronto's surplus tax yields is destined for poor regions, of which Canada has many, that are unable to pay their own way. This is understood as a price of equity or fraternity, of national unity and peace, and as a rough justice rendered indirectly from large corporations whose taxpaying head offices may be in Toronto or its region, but which profitably exploit natural resources nationwide. All that, however, doesn't alter the fact that not enough resources return for municipal reinvestment. Murray points out that Winnipeg can't scrape up the modest sums needed for adequate repair of winter-damaged pavements and curbs. The inadequacy of resources for social investment penalizes children who need educations that were unnecessary when youngsters were destined for farm and mining labor, logging and fishing, or servants' jobs.

Toronto's current public poverty is artificial, deliberately imposed by policies that in Canada are called neoconservatism. In America, a similar ideology is known as reinvented government or the Washington consensus. In Britain it takes the name of Thatcherism. Internationally, much the same set of beliefs and policies is recognizable as "economic reforms demanded by the International Monetary Fund."

At the core of this intellectual phenomenon now shaping much (but not all) of Western culture is a moralistic belief that each public service or amenity should directly earn enough to support its cost. Thus each school is supposed to earn enough to support itself, through fees of some kind or through profit-making arrangements such as sale to a corporation of monopolistic rights to vend soft drinks and snacks. Such arrangements are called public-private partnerships (PPP, or P3) and are much encouraged by neoconservatives and most boards of trade. Each artist is supposed to earn enough in his or her own lifetime to prove the art's fitness to exist. Hospitals, transit systems, and orchestras are scorned as freeloaders seeking handouts if they can't directly pay their way or, better yet, make a profit either for tax collectors or for a corporate partner. Greed becomes culturally admired as competence, and false or unrealistic promises as cleverness.

To be sure, neoconservative ideologues are selective in their social and economic choices for worthiness to survive and flourish. They subsidize professional sports stadiums, automotive assembly plants, roads, and other preferences, with tax breaks and other benefits.

In Canada, neoconservative governments display their success in the form of tax breaks or tax rebates, primarily benefiting rich taxpayers under the assumption (or excuse) that they will invest the money in job creation. What the cuts do, rather, at least for a time or two, is buy elections. In 2000, an election year, our provincial government sent tax-cut rebates of $200 to most taxpayers. I received one. This is why school librarians can't be paid, or music teachers and teachers of

English as a second language. It is why there are no low-rent rooming houses for old men. Most families receiving those checks pay more than $200 in such added expenses—depending on circumstances—as higher rents, higher transit costs, and new recreation and tuition fees. The tax cuts' chief benefit, as far as I can see, is the emotional satisfaction they bring to ideologues.

Virtually all ideologues, of any variety, are fearful and insecure, which is why they are drawn to ideologies that promise prefabricated answers for all circumstances. Every society contains such people. But they can exert considerable power only when they control public purse strings which are not subject to the principles of subsidiarity and fiscal accountability. In the case of Canada, that flaw is actually written into the country's constitution, but in various forms and degrees it occurs just about everywhere.

When Canada's constitution was formulated and adopted in 1867, as the British North America Act, a document of the English Parliament, most of the country's scanty population lived in rural hamlets based on trapping, fishing, logging, or meager agriculture and stock raising. There were no cities other than Montreal and Quebec City, the French capital, both of which had fallen to the English by their defeat of the French in war, and embryonic Toronto. The few substantial settlements were narrowly based company towns such as fur-trading posts, or frontier military garrisons or tiny market towns that depended directly on the rural economies.

The constitution did not recognize these socially and economically feeble settlements as institutions of government. It bracketed them, instead, with asylums and taverns, as dependent wards of the provinces, and they were allowed to levy only property taxes. This was probably not a bad idea at a time when they were capable of no more than maintaining unpaved streets, fighting fires (usually by self-organized volunteers), providing rudimentary sewers and wells, and operating jails for holding drunks and other disorderly characters who got out of hand.

Now half the Canadian population lives in the country's five largest cities; another 30 percent live in settlements with populations of ten thousand or more, mostly in the suburbs or exurbs of large cities. The Canadian rural economy, including mining, logging, and fishing as well as agriculture, accounts for only about 3 percent of gross domestic product. The rest of the economy depends on tourism, popular arts and fine arts, technological research and enterprises, construction, wholesale and retail services, publishing and printing, manufacturing, and health, education, and other government-supported services and amenities.

Canadian municipalities are no longer country-bumpkin villages. The expertise and creative abilities they contain put provincial and federal legislatures and agencies to shame, as Toronto demonstrated with its infill assisted housing. City populations possess diversified abilities for identifying, diagnosing, and solving local shortcomings and needs. Even municipalities that are still small are sufficiently sophisticated to know where to find knowledgeable help. Yet the anachronistic provincial-municipal wardship arrangements still hold. When the constitution was patriated in 1982—declared a Canadian instead of a British document—guarantees of basic civil rights were added, but nothing was done to change the relationship of municipalities with provinces.

Healthy municipalities do not march in lockstep. At a

given time, each has its own needs and may also have its own particular opportunities for innovative solutions. These opportunities can be very valuable. Central planning, whether by leftists or conservatives, draws too little on local knowledge and creativity, stifles innovations, and is inefficient and costly because it is circuitous. It bypasses intimate and varied knowledge directly fed back into the system.

Between the mid-1950s and the early 1990s, Toronto did well on the whole, with several significant episodes of city import replacing during those forty years, which enhanced both its property tax base and its reservoirs of diverse exportable goods and services.

However, beneath the tranquil and prosperous surface, much was going wrong. The adaptation by the city to new and increased demands upon it was to load onto its property tax costs that were unforeseeable in 1867. These included, for instance, costs of inspections of restaurant kitchens, canneries, bottlers, and other food processors; health inspection of homes for the elderly; welfare costs; policing against telephone and door-to-door fraudsters; lifeguards for beaches and instructors for school swimming pools; archivists; recreational and educational programs in parks; salaries for horticulturists to combat the spread of diseases in street and park trees, and for biologists to track outbreaks of rabies and fevers in urban wildlife; experiments with recycling and other waste management schemes; discouragement of hate crimes and other expressions of intolerance; encouragement of ethnic celebrations; and so on, all part of the fabric of modern urban life.

Many costs of urban life and urban infrastructures are most equitably levied according to ability to pay; others are most equitably related to expansion of the economy. These taxes are reserved for the so-called senior governments. So municipalities have loaded everything onto the property tax, decade after decade. As with the camel's load that was increased a straw at a time, along came the straws that threatened to break the back of this system. Finally, increases in property tax assessments on small businesses—laundries, restaurants, retail stores—were becoming so heavy as added operating costs that they threatened to bankrupt many establishments and put them out of business, along with their suppliers and employees. Proposed separation of public financial responsibilities, some for residential property taxpayers and some for business taxpayers, sounded like a plausible way out of the impasse. But it wasn't. The division itself was deceptive and inequitable (so much for fiscal accountability) and gave more power than ever to the province to micromanage the city, with the destructive kinds of results I have touched on.

The province had also introduced an additional layer of government, called Metro, which ostensibly was to coordinate governance of the city proper with its inner suburbs. Metro was rigged so that the city's heart could and would be outvoted on decisions when the car-dependent and community-deficient suburban subcultures conflicted with the city subculture, which happened constantly. Metro government was one tedious wrangle after another. The ill-assorted parts fought about their shares of residential property tax assessments, and began undermining the transit system by insisting that it bear the costs of suburban routes that couldn't pay for themselves; the "solution" was to force transit services in the city, which more than paid their costs, to subsidize inefficient routes until city transit was bled dry.

Conflicting financial and social elements in the Metro

arrangement became truly catastrophic in 1998 when the dysfunctional parts were amalgamated under a single new City of Toronto government, in defiance of provincially unauthorized local referendums opposing it. The province promised that amalgamation would save money. It didn't. It was expensive for many reasons, some unavoidable, some irresponsible, some apparently corrupt, all of them deplorable. From this time on, Toronto's deterioration became visible and enraging, with surprising rapidity. Whether tourism began declining because the city had become less attractive or for other reasons was unknown because Toronto had been forestalled (see p. 104) from getting funds to experiment with providing information for tourists and gathering information from them.

Some worried and angry Canadian citizens argue that large cities and their metropolitan areas should break away from existing provinces and form new provinces of their own (under the existing federal government), thereby bridging the gulf that separates public resources from subsidiarity and fiscal accountability. They may be right. But it seems like reaching for a sledgehammer to drive a tack.

A gentler remedy could be for the federal government to allot, as of right, a share of its income-tax yields to municipalities or, again as of right, a portion of the federal goods and services tax, which is a value-added tax under another name. Municipalities would thus share in the investments made possible by the rewards of economic expansion. Perhaps best would be a mixture of the two allotments. Since they would go to municipalities as of right, without strings, the so-called senior governments could cease trying to micromanage and to standardize municipal policies and governance. Standardization is the parent of stagnation.

When I had an opportunity to discuss this revenue-sharing possibility with Mr. Paul Martin, who at the time was federal finance minister and who has become Canada's new prime minister, he first dismissed the suggestion out of hand with the excuse that the constitution doesn't allow it. I pointed out that nothing in the constitution forbids sharing the yields from forms of taxation that did not even exist until generations after the adoption of the British North America Act, and that the federal government already allots income-tax shares, or points, as they are called, to the provinces.

When I saw a shadow pass over his expressive and attentive face, I assumed he was glumly contemplating tax increases. I remarked that sharing income tax with municipalities would not entail higher taxes because it would be only fair to subtract equivalent funds from allotments to provinces to care for their erstwhile dependents. Possibly it was a mistake to mention this, although he is a smart man and would surely soon have looked at this side of the equation for himself. He quickly shot out, "*Impossible!* Everybody wants money!" bringing our taxation discussion to a halt. Our vantage points, and therefore our views, were different. A reform that meant to me correction of a grave social and economic disconnection that is unraveling the country's complex modern functional networks meant to him, I saw as his ears and face closed up, a nasty power struggle with the premiers of ten provinces who are determined to keep their power instead of sharing it with their more knowledgeable, anachronistic wards.

Perhaps to cheer or placate me, he told me that he intended to announce a program of federal grants enabling municipalities to install light-rail public transit. Now it was my turn to demur. I told him that unfortunate experiences already showed that fixed transit routes were expensive failures when they were not preceded by evidence of sufficient demand. Underused routes not only are a drain on transit systems but are ill-suited as contributors to the needs and convenience of users. In the past, designers of transit systems had usually chosen to locate rail routes by observing which bus routes were most heavily used, a pragmatic method that worked well in Toronto and elsewhere. After it was apparently lost to transit engineers' memories in the 1960s, Toronto and a number of other cities, among them Atlanta, Buffalo, Detroit, and Chicago, tried rail routes justified by other goals and these have proved unable to pull their weights, literally or figuratively. They don't have enough passengers. I asserted that a prudent program to promote transit must be flexible enough to encourage experiments with routes, should that be what a city wanted to do, and possibly experiment with bus sizes, before settling on fixed rail routes. Why not specify grants for transit? I wondered aloud. Why specify from on high what form the transit must take?

I was too tactful to mention the hazards of being out of touch with specific needs, nor my suspicion that he found a light-rail grant program attractive because it would be a federal goody to extend to Bombardier, a Canadian multinational corporation that manufactures streetcars, with headquarters in Montreal, and that this benefit would be well received by Quebec voters, ever a pressing concern of the federal government, but these thoughts went quickly through my head.

As he saw my ears and face close up, he pointed out that the mayors of every large city had asked for light-rail transit grants. I told him that I had attended the meetings where they arrived at this unanimity; they reasoned that asking for light-rail grants was politically more realistic than asking for other kinds of public transit equipment or more general transit help, such as grants for operating costs, the most desperate need in some municipalities.

Mr. Martin perfunctorily conceded that flexibility might be worth taking into consideration. Again I saw that our points of view were different. What he could contemplate as attractive bonanzas for clamoring cities and perhaps for complaining corporations producing rails and streetcars, I feared as foregone fiascoes.

It being my turn to try to restore harmony, I remarked that we both had, in common, concern for the common good. He could have replied, but was too polite to do so, that everybody claims a desire to promote the common good. The common good is an abstraction, whose construction and collapse play out in many concrete decisions and acts.

Declining voter turnouts and increasing disdain among polled members of the public for politicians (and their promises) are evidence that people in a number of Western countries have concluded that voting is a waste of effort. That increasing numbers of voters act this way in advanced democracies, where the sense of civic responsibility should be strongest, indicates popular disconnection from Lincoln's government "of the people, by the people, for the people." Pigeonholing that ideal as irrelevant or unattainable means *losing it.* That is how weakening of cultural webs leads to further weakening.

While Canada has the unique constitutional flaws I have mentioned, flaws with surprisingly similar results plague American municipalities. As this is written, in spring of 2003, the mayor of New York, Michael Bloomberg, is locked into a budget combat with the governor of New York State, George Pataki. The mayor says that to overcome a threatened city budget deficit of nearly $4 billion, he needs to impose a tax on commuters' pay earned in the city. The governor says he won't allow it. The mayor says his alternative is to reduce numbers of police recruits; lay off sanitation workers; slash overtime pay of firemen; close swimming pools; drastically cut staff for child services, health and mental hygiene, services for the homeless, and after-school educational and recreational programs; and reduce or perhaps eliminate weekend take-home meals for poor elderly people. Of course he has enumerated service cuts he judges would be most politically unpopular. The governor points to his own forthcoming state budget deficit of $10 billion, but in any case, like the U.S. president, he is an ideological tax cutter, regardless of deficits, layoffs, and loss of services. It all sounds very familiar to a Canadian.

Colonial possessions of European and Asian empires used to be the most deprived of the benefits of subsidiarity and fiscal responsibility. Since World War II, poor countries receiving foreign aid are in that unenviable position. Dumbed-down resources move through the stratosphere from rich sovereign governments—or the World Bank and the International Monetary Fund, which are much the same as rich sovereign states—to poor sovereign governments for disbursement. Running like a sad refrain through half a century and billions of dollars of waste and disappointment, and often outright harm, is the lament "The aid didn't reach those for whom it was intended."

The unintended consequences have been many. Peasants

have been pauperized as they were evicted from ancestral lands for dams accompanied by promises of prosperity through electricity and attraction of foreign corporations with jobs. Where prosperity failed to materialize, unpayable national debts were forgiven on condition of reforms which themselves increased poverty and upheaval. A book could be written about dysfunctional, dumbed-down, out-of-touch foreign aid. Indeed, many books have been, some by appalled outsiders, some by rueful insiders and participants. Good intentions are not lacking; subsidiarity and fiscal accountability are.

Aid failures promote instability and terrorism. Some of the ugly scenes to which we have become accustomed, such as crowds of screaming young men in city streets; boys throwing stones at armed soldiers and police; lethally armed child soldiers organized into marauding bands of robbers and murderers; carnage of innocent people by angry, vengeful suicide bombers—these are harvests of many complex failures with many causes. Among those causes are our culture's profound failure to make practical realities of the principles of subsidiarity and financial accountability. Throwing money at programs omitting those principles is no solution. Legal power not based on those principles is no solution. Blaming victims is not enlightening; after all, in even the most prosperous and fortunate countries, those of the OECD, nobody knows how to fix the lacks of subsidiarity and fiscal accountability, and if we in North America are unable to fix this problem for ourselves, of course we can't fix it for others.

CHAPTER SIX

Self-Policing Subverted

Members of learned professions have traditionally been regarded by themselves and others as capable of responsibly regulating, and even policing, themselves through oversight by bar associations, law societies, state boards of medicine, colleges of physicians and surgeons, medical associations, institutes of architects, engineering societies, institutes of certified or chartered accountants, and the like. These people not only enjoy status as educated experts; they are seen as establishment figures with stakes in maintaining stability, honesty, and good order for the common welfare. They are trusted to discipline or strip professional status from such frauds, brutes, and psychopaths as make their ways into high-minded professional ranks.

Historically, professional insistence on self-regulation, and social trust in professionals' accountability, hark back to ancient priesthoods, probably the first learned societies. Priestly history echoes into modern times. Governments and priesthoods have often come into conflict over clerical demands for exemption from civil regulation, especially when clergies' demands have overflowed into demands to prescribe or dictate for others too. This sort of conflict was at issue in the separation of the Anglican Church from the Roman Catholic Church under Henry VIII in England: it remains a very live issue in Israel and in some Islamic countries to this day.

Self-regulation and self-policing are different, although they overlap and blur. "Self-regulation" refers mainly to the internal affairs of professional groups. For example, architects' professional institutes typically mandate the fees their members charge clients, with these customarily set at standard percentages of the total cost of projects, on a sliding scale. This is roughly realistic; the larger a project, the more work is usually entailed, from initial programming and design, through working drawings, specifications, tendering, and construction supervision. However, architects of outstanding originality and conscientiousness tend to lavish effort on small projects in amounts that render standard percentages unrealistic. As usual in life, one size does not fit all.

In many other commercial activities, mutually agreed-upon fees among competitors for clients would be deemed illegal collusion in restraint of trade. The architects' rationale is that if fee shaving is eschewed as legitimate competition, then artistry, skill, and competence can be concentrated upon as competitive factors instead. In a field like architecture—part art, and also very much a matter of public safety and public amenity—competitive quality surely cannot be written off as a bad thing.

Another form of architects' self-regulation is to ban criticism of another's work, especially criticism that can be heard or read by outsiders. This is why one reads few critical reviews by architects of new buildings, in comparison with reviews by writers, say, of books, dramas, and film, or by musicians of musical compositions and performances. Architects' mutual protection from adverse notice extends, when possible, to criticism by outsiders as well. When I was hired as an editor and writer by an architectural journal, the editor in chief gave me quickly to understand that I must shun critical comment. Otherwise, he explained, not only would our magazine stir up an unpleasant ruckus, but all architects, including those whose work was most interesting, would refuse us information and permission to publish their designs—a death sentence for the magazine.

We made quality distinctions, of course. If there were good ideas and useful lessons in an ungainly or mean piece of work, we emphasized the good points and ignored their context; but this was rare. Almost always we published only proposals, buildings, or projects we could unreservedly admire, or that the editor in chief unreservedly admired, ignoring others. So for an architect to get his work published in a journal where it could be seen by clients was a compliment, rather like a low-key award. We were attuned to reputations within the profession, and we bowed obsequiously to fashion (a word we never mentioned; architecture has styles, not fashions), as did architects themselves. Leafing through design and architectural journals a half century later, I see that they still abide by the familiar restrictions.

Only after an architect was dead and his office had dissolved, or so much time had elapsed that objectivity was deemed feasible, could critical lessons be learned from our magazine or other architectural journals, which were all in the same bind as ours. Like architects themselves, we were unable to pursue educational work we might have undertaken for enlightenment of the public, clients, students, and other architects.

Somewhat counterbalancing this omission, however, is educational work undertaken by many local institutes of architects. They research problems that members have in common, hold discussions, listen to invited speakers—some of them critical—and maintain mutual education committees on various building and construction types, such as schools, hospitals, civic buildings, and street designs. This would hardly be possible if members felt seriously threatened by one another.

Professional self-regulation extends to many more subjects than the two I've mentioned, depending on the profession. All variations have the self-interest of members at their core, usually sincerely construed as advancement of the profession itself. A frequently adopted regulation dictates whether members may advertise commercially, and if so, subject to what rules. Recruits are frequently required to pass examinations composed and supervised by the professional body. These are usually more difficult and comprehensive than examinations recruits have already passed at the conclusion of university studies, and I have never heard of corrupt decisions on grades. These examinations antedate the current debasement of university credentials, having been instituted in the nineteenth or very early twentieth centuries, at a time when a young man could get a legal education by reading law under the personal supervision of a judge or experienced lawyer, an architectural education by apprenticeship in an established studio, or even a medical education (usually shockingly inadequate) by observing and assisting a physician or surgeon. A side effect of professional examinations is that they control the number of recruits admitted into the profession. To have too many, relative to current work available, threatens the prosperity of all; to have too few reduces the supply of low-paid juniors articled or interned for specific periods as apprentices.

On the whole, professional self-regulation seems well tolerated in Western European and North American culture because it is confined largely to internal professional concerns that are not commonly seen as menacing, and which, in any case, the public knows little about. Furthermore, it is hard to imagine what other institutions of society could serve as regulators of internal professional affairs. The likely alternatives are probably burdensome and irrelevant bureaucracies, or else lack of regulation, and also perhaps demoralization of professionals— not a good thing to risk.

Self-policing is touchier and more problematic than self-regulation because it must combat fraud or other outright crimes, and also misbehavior that borders on the criminal. It overlaps with self-regulation most obviously when malfeasance is covered up in the interest of professional solidarity and the profession's public reputation. There is no quicker way for a profession to lose public respect than to cover up, institutionally, for members who have done arrant wrong, a lesson that priesthoods are learning once again, and this could mean that the Roman Catholic priesthood's self-regulating rules about celibacy and the gender of members need revision.

Mutual protection can be more subtly discerned when professions are notably reluctant or tardy in coming to grips with self-policing responsibilities to which they nevertheless cling tenaciously. Although this is less raw than covering up, tardiness too arouses public alarm and condemnation. Notorious examples are brutality toward aboriginal children or orphans by Protestant missionaries or Catholic nuns, and cases of medical malpractice, quite rightly seen as indefensible when diseases and even deaths continue while a medical association dilly-dallies, sometimes for years after credible complaints and damning evidence have been brought to its attention. In these cases, the protection of members from harassment or false accusations, and the protection of victims from harm, have become so unbalanced that it would be better for a profession to give up on self-policing and leave crime and punishment to police and courts, rather than to bishops and professional disciplinary committees.

In cover-ups or unreasonable tardiness, three different transgressions are often involved. First, the actual crime: the embezzlement, the malpractice, the child abuse, the bribe taking or giving. Second, the cover-up, involving individuals of considerable power or influence who were not involved personally in the initial wrongdoing, but whose sense of loyalty is stronger than their attachment to honesty and openness. Since exaggerated loyalty may be the very quality that gives such people power and influence in their institutions, it is hard to know what can be done about loyalty as self-serving weakness. Third, the near crime of hoodwinking police with false assurances that all is well.

Ah, the police. Police officers form organizations too, which are the most self-protective of all. Even when police don't organize into police benevolent associations, they are exaggeratedly protective of one another. Police can seldom be depended on to police themselves. Their most common forms of crime are bribe taking, brutality, and bearing false witness. When police crimes are unmasked, it is usually done by investigative journalists, sometimes helped by brave informants from the inside and increasingly helped by scientists such as forensic biologists and demographers. The standard reform attempted is a new layer of oversight: a civilian review board to receive and deal with accusations by the public. Short public memory—every scandal is only a nine-day wonder—and sincere but sentimentalized public appreciation of the risks police run tend to undermine civilian review boards as long-term remedies.

Most sovereignties have in reserve high-level, exceptional investigative procedures and enforcement powers—for instance, congressional investigations in the United States, and crown inquiries in Canada and other Western monarchies. But these oversights leave much crime unattended to, especially commercial crime.

Commercial enterprises, as we all know, form associations to press their self-interests on governments and to present clean faces in public: manufacturers', home builders', small-business, and tobacco growers' associations; chambers of commerce, boards of trade, business improvement districts, and so on. However, these differ from self-regulating professional organizations, perhaps because business associations are not culturally descended from priesthoods. At any rate, they lack the expectations of themselves that learned professions assume, nor does the public place trust in business associations as it has traditionally done in the learned professions. Self-policing and self-regulation have never been typical business responsibilities.

Advanced cultures are usually sophisticated enough, or have been sophisticated enough at some point in their pasts, to realize that foxes shouldn't be relied on to guard henhouses. Civil legislation and courts take responsibility for adjudicating such commercial matters as contracts, rights to intellectual properties, and governance of limited liability corporations (and, indeed, permission to form corporations in the first place). Uses of force or fraud by commercial enterprises are, without exception, defined as crimes. Without safeguards against them, trading would degenerate into raiding and extortion.

Some forms of business fraud are comparatively easy to police: effective combat against short weight and counterfeit coins, for instance, is very ancient, extending back into prehistoric times. New frauds are forever emerging, followed by ways to detect them.

The most gigantic types of business fraud cannot be physically tested by inspectors, as adulterated butter can; or confiscated, like tainted meat; or recalled by manufacturers, like brakes with life-threatening flaws, or hazardous toys.

Columns of fraudulent figures, attesting to the robust financial condition of a company that may actually be on the verge of bankruptcy, are contrived either by falsifying expenses or by exaggerating income. To prevent false financial reporting, governments have long required corporations, partnerships, and many other enterprises, including those claiming to be nonprofit or charitable, to employ independent accountants to audit their financial statements and attest to the statements' truth and accuracy.

Members of one of the learned professions, certified public accountants (in Canada called chartered accountants), have been trusted to oversee and guarantee honest financial reporting by business, which is why business at large is trusted. That is the principal function of accountants in civilized societies. Businesses themselves benefit from honest accounting; it combats embezzlement and alerts them to their own wastes, inefficiencies, and competitive weaknesses and strengths. When a profession with responsibilities like that goes rotten, it is a cultural and economic nightmare.

The financial debacle in 2001 at Enron, a huge and complex energy-trading firm with headquarters in Houston, Texas, was a severe shock to the U.S. economy. False accounting inflated Enron's apparent profits and concealed its all-too-real losses. As the press has fully reported, this maintained unjustifiably high prices per share of Enron stock long enough for the corporation's top executives to reap fortunes in the millions of dollars from sales of stock to which they had been granted options as part of their generous compensation. When the corporation went into bankruptcy soon afterward, the value of the stock plunged.

Many of Enron's ordinary workers, who had been misled along with the rest of the public, abruptly lost their retirement savings. So did savers and investors in many other pension funds, and thousands of small investors in mutual funds that held Enron stock. Enron auditors attempted to cover up evidence of accounting fraud by destroying incriminating documents. The executives who profited so handsomely in such a timely manner denied knowledge of the company's finances, briefly managing to shield themselves from liability.

This was followed early in 2002 by an epidemic of bankruptcies in huge corporations. The deceptive accounting in each case was not necessarily arranged by auditors themselves, but by consultants whose services the auditors supplied. The tricks used were so arcane and elaborate that they all but passed understanding. The definition of madness is loss of connection with reality. By that definition, this was accounting gone mad; in olden times it would have been said that transgressing members of the profession had sold their souls to the devil.

However the rot set in, it did not happen overnight. It began at least as far back as the mid-1980s, as a consequence of that decade's frenzies of mergers and takeovers, which created unprecedentedly gigantic and unmanageable business combines. Some shaky corporations that were overloaded with debts incurred for acquisitions, and were desperate for further financing, took to paying auditors for "solvency letters" untruthfully assuring lenders of the corporations' soundness as borrowers. News of the letters, and their price of half a million dollars each, became public in 1987 owing to a lawsuit concerning a bankrupt company that had used such a letter. Accountants, speaking anonymously, told *The Wall Street Journal* that mergers had so much reduced the numbers of corporate clients that auditors had to rustle up additional sources of income for themselves, such as the production of solvency letters. In addition, they said, corporate clients threatened to fire auditors if demanded letters were not forthcoming.

Auditors themselves embarked upon frenzied merging and consolidating. Perhaps this was defensive, to rival bullying clients' sizes and muscle. The result was five enormous multinational accounting firms, each employing tens of thousands of certified public accountants and related consultants. One of these accounting ogres, Arthur Andersen, was Enron's disgraced auditor. Because of its ruined reputation, the Andersen firm broke up and went out of business. But its fragments survive and have found work in many European countries, as well as North America. All five of the giants have now been mentioned in the press as alleged collaborators with corporations whose columns of figures couldn't support their houses of cards.

In the meantime, the culture had cast up a new tactic, plausible denial, for use by deceivers. This is a preemptive preparation for future crimes and cover-ups. Underlings doing the actual deceiving or other wrongs are careful not to inform superiors (in writing or in front of witnesses or eavesdroppers) of what they are doing, in order to shield superiors from accountability. This tactic seems to have been invented in the U.S. Central Intelligence Agency (CIA) but perhaps it originated in foreign secret police or spy organizations. It first came into prominent—indeed, prestigious—use in North America when it was adopted by two presidents: Richard Nixon, who invoked plausible denial, unsuccessfully, to defend himself from culpability in the Watergate scandal, and Ronald Reagan, who used it successfully to shield himself in the Iran-Contra scandals. The current president, George W. Bush, has used it to defend himself against allegations of unreported stock trading, an illegality the president has acknowledged but self-excused on grounds of ignorance of the law. He reportedly gained $16 million from the transaction, shortly before he became president. Speaking of plausible denial, a former chairman of the Securities and Exchange Commission has called it "a game of nods and winks."

Schools of business are not blameless. These institutions are trusted to educate certified public accountants and the businessmen and businesswomen who can be expected to employ them. In the summer of 2002, three of America's most prestigious universities held a special three-day seminar, at the University of Chicago, for some eighty executives drawn from the country's largest multinational corporations. The purpose was to offer them guidance concerning accounting malpractice. One might suppose, offhand, that the advice would be "Don't do it; don't allow it." Not at all. A business

journalist from *The New York Times,* who was also in atten-
dance, reported that, instead, the university mentors warned
their high-level students against candor. "They were told that
if they were forced to give a legal deposition in the aftermath
of a scandal, they should not volunteer any information":
Don't ask, don't tell.

Behind the success of plausible denial is an already long-
standing North American disconnection from reality: the
substitution of image for substance. The idea is that a pre-
sentable image makes substance immaterial. All that glitters *is*
gold. This probably began with the glorification of literary
and social celebrities during the latter nineteenth century, although it was remarked even earlier as an American tendency.
False image making has become a very big business throughout North America and is a staple of the U.S. government.
Legions of hired liars labor to disconnect reality from all
manner of images—images of personalities, of legislation, of
corporations, of places, and of activities. Spin doctors, virtu-
osos of deceptive image making and damage control, have become authoritative spokespersons in political campaigns and
troubled institutions, able not only to disconnect reality but
to construct new reality. If that sounds confusing about the
reality of reality, it is; that is the purpose of spin-doctoring.

Dishonesty and greed, which I have been discussing, are
easily condemned; accountants themselves know these are
exploitative and wrong as means for carrying on trade and
government. But there are deeper and more puzzling issues in
accounting nowadays; accountants grappling with them do
not know what are the right or wrong ways to deal with them,
and neither does anyone else. Plenty of legitimate puzzles demand attention from smart accountants.

One of the elementary realities in accounting is the distinction between capital assets and operating expenses. Capital assets are bankable: money can be borrowed to buy or build them; if the owner defaults on interest or repayments, the lender can foreclose on the assets and resell them, perhaps to another borrower. This derives from the traditional concepts of capital, based on such assets as land, buildings, ships and their cargoes, and, since the industrial revolution, production equipment. But a body of knowledge or a piece of information can be capital; even something as gossamer as an idea can sometimes be intellectual capital.

The traditional concept of capital has already broken down when an educational credential is conceived of as collateral, like a farm, crop, or machine that can be borrowed against to obtain it; but in case of default a credential cannot be foreclosed and resold like a farm, crop, or machine.

Suppose a city plans to upgrade a waste recycling program to increase wealth and reduce costs of transporting and storing wastes. This entails educating producers of wastes and furnishing them with low-priced composters and other receptacles. Are those expenses capital costs, against which the city can borrow? Or are they operating expenses, which can't exist until relevant capital assets exist? This is not a hypothetical accounting issue. The question has arisen in the 2003 Toronto budget and has pitted city accountants against one another.

The phrases "human capital," "social capital," and "cultural capital" are glibly spoken. These represent concepts about real and powerful assets, more indispensable for wealth creation and well-being in modern societies than traditional bankable capital—but difficult or impossible to handle in traditional accounting terms. "Development costs" doesn't really cover them.

They can produce wealth during their development and use. They consist of knowledge, skills, and social and legal working assumptions—all of which are culturally transmitted—possessed by a population.

How does one budget the inventory of an enterprise that, by contract, retains ownership of part of its sold products, such as durable material remaining in a camera, floor covering, or an appliance, so the maker can reclaim, recondition, and resell the fraction with long-lasting value after the perishable part of the product is consumed? Again, this is not a hypothetical issue; it has already emerged, and if this manufacturing/recycling tactic is financially successful—which depends in part upon good guidance from accountants—the practice may spread.

Arrested accounting is unhelpful for unprecedented financial concepts. The need for innovation in accounting practices is hopeful evidence of promising economic developments. Evidence that accountants can meet the needs of a vigorously developing economy competently and also cleave to honesty is not yet in. No doubt, needed changes will occur in gradual, evolutionary steps as occasion requires—or not at all. The profession is split among those who argue the wisdom of adopting pioneering accounting rules, and those who condemn them. This is not a matter of good guys versus bad guys; the virtues of both schools of thought are needed to facilitate innovative solutions to current problems. The vices of both schools of thought are old and tiresome: fraud, image making, contrived denial, spin-doctoring.

CHAPTER SEVEN

Unwinding Vicious Spirals

Interlocked problems, intractably spiraling downward and joining with other problems into amalgamated declines, are daunting but not supernatural. They are tangible consequences of tangible mistakes and misfortunes. Homelessness and unaffordable housing, and their ramifications, have direct and tangible roots in the Great Depression of the 1930s and in the war years that followed: people could not afford to build in the 1930s, and during the war both construction materials and skilled workers drained into urgent war work instead of into postponable civilian needs.

Another tangible mark of those fifteen years, which seems to be less vividly remembered, was growing shabbiness and dilapidation. Not that there had previously been any shortage of shanties, of walls rotting for lack of paint, or of roofs leaking for lack of patches, but fifteen years elapsed when owners who would normally have renovated existing buildings, or at least maintained them, let things deteriorate; they had little choice. What had been pockets of dilapidation became shockingly larger.

The major way in which households hit by the Depression got by was doubling up: overcrowding. Cheap places for rent were abundant. In Manhattan, where I was living at the time, nothing was easier than finding an apartment of whatever size one specified, in almost whichever neighborhood one specified. That is why a stenographer earning $12 a week, joined by one or two other women of similarly slender means, could be offered so many choices of financially feasible quarters with living room, kitchen, bath, and one or two bedrooms. Stamina to examine dwellings on offer ran out sooner than the list of offerings. But abundance was deceptive; one household's gain was at the expense of another household's loss of its own dwelling.

In 1941, the Manhattan housing supply had tightened. That year the real estate agent could come up with only three good possibilities instead of twenty or thirty, and I was glad to have the extra weekly dollars from my move into a $15-a-week secretarial job in a steel-distributing company. The tightened supply was not evident all over America. In Scranton, this first taste of incipient prosperity emptied even more houses—some very desirable—than the Depression had emptied, because Scranton was not acquiring new jobs. To find them, thousands of residents left, some for New York, as I previously had, but most for Bridgeport, Connecticut, and the Baltimore area to take work in brass foundries, steel rolling-mills, and other heavy industries. Pioneers among these migrants took in later Scranton migrants, until employers saw to it that tracts of cramped houses, meeting minimum standards, were thrown up and reserved for workers in war plants.

Scranton and a few other pockets of persistent economic stagnation notwithstanding, rental dwellings rapidly became more costly and scarce almost everywhere. In Manhattan, my husband and I took in two friends as roomers; they helped carry the rising rent. One, the wife of a naval officer who was soon to serve in the South Pacific, put aside work on her Ph.D. history of the cutlery industry in the Connecticut River Valley to introduce women factory workers migrating from the rural South to the intricacies of collective bargaining. The other, a teacher from Nova Scotia, worked in a super-secret Canadian and British intelligence office that purchased necessities for spies and commando raiders and served as an American base for European code-breakers and other valuable geniuses. But we learned never so much as a hint of this until she came for a visit about ten years after the war had ended, so unostentatiously silent had she been about the nature of her work; we had not even known that she worked in a Rockefeller Center skyscraper, or her telephone number there.

By the end of the war, the affordable housing shortage in New York and elsewhere was so acute, and evictions were so alarmingly common, that the shortage had become a crisis. Public policies to address it fell into three approaches: (1) court-enforced rent controls; (2) slum clearance and subsidized housing projects for low-income veterans and others whose incomes qualified them for preference; and (3) long-term low-interest mortgages, guaranteed by government agencies, to encourage construction for home ownership. The second and third approaches had been tentatively begun on small scales during the Depression, then had been largely halted during the war, and resumed robustly after the war.

Rent controls helped check the avarice of profiteering land-lords. Evictions for inability to meet rent increases diminished or halted. But otherwise, on balance, rent control was counter-productive, because it did nothing to correct the core problem, the lack of new or decently maintained affordable housing, the missing supply that was a legacy of fifteen years of depression and war. Some landlords, who claimed that their buildings could no longer earn enough to pay their property taxes and their heating and other maintenance costs, which was some-times true and sometimes not, stopped paying taxes and taking responsibility for their buildings, leaving them to deteriorate further, be looted, or be occupied by drug dealers, a newly burgeoning phenomenon in the city. Abandoned buildings in New York, which eventually numbered in the thousands, were usually in areas that had become so dilapidated during the De-pression and the war that owners judged (erroneously) that they could never recover value in the future, and refused to correct fire, structural, and other serious safety violations. Other land-lords found loopholes in the law, for example converting former family-sized apartments into several tiny units, locally known as birth-control apartments. These looked good in the dwelling statistics and won court approvals for rent increases that, in ag-gregate, raised building yields, but meant only hardship and loss of community for evicted families and placed still more de-mand on the inadequate supply. Hidden but appreciable costs of rent controls were the efforts and legal costs that landlords devoted to combat against tenants and their advocates (combats which the landlords did not always win) and the savings and ef-forts that tenants put into battles (which they did not always win). A social cost was the conversion of formerly tranquil areas into continuous battlefields of predators versus prey.

Slum clearance was even more counterproductive. This approach seemed superficially plausible because solid maintenance and renovation work had unavoidably been neglected during the Depression and war years, and the neglect showed. Dilapidated areas were designated for future clearance and replacement, it was promised, by "decent, safe and sanitary dwellings," the routine reassurance of planners and politicians at the time. Slum designations were reinforced by bank "redlining," meaning denial of property loans, not on account of poor creditworthiness of applicants or even the condition of the buildings themselves, but on account of location in a neighborhood designated for clearance. Loan famine added to shelter famine. Redlining was one reason buildings were abandoned by owners.

Theoretically, people displaced from their homes by slum clearance were to be accommodated in the new, subsidized buildings if (or while) their incomes were low enough to qualify them. But things seldom worked out that way. Planning fads and architectural fashions of the time emphasized the desirability of empty, open spaces; thus replacement buildings usually provided fewer affordable dwellings than the numbers destroyed. Years passed between evictions from the old and construction of the new. During these periods, when housing had simply been subtracted, not added, redlined districts and expropriated or abandoned buildings were sometimes used for relocation. Evicted people were stuffed into them as transient and deprived populations, which led to further building and community deterioration, both physical and social.

When the new slum-replacement housing was built, it didn't wear well, physically or socially. The projects were so badly sited and designed, so autocratically run, and so discouraging to wholesome community life that soon they began to be abandoned by people who could find any other accommodation. The explosive demolition by St. Louis housing officials of a building in the huge, notorious Pruitt-Igoe housing project became a spectacular symbol of slum-clearance failures. By the mid-1990s, an estimated eleven thousand units of unsalvageable subsidized housing for the poor were being demolished in the United States each year. Only about four thousand replacement units were being constructed per year. Salvage attempts were made but were seldom well conceived or successful.

After 1949, the many governmental attacks on affordable housing were intensified by land clearances of low-cost housing for urban renewal projects, intended for middle- and high-income residents, and after 1956 by subsidized highway programs, all of which targeted so-called slums when they could be found. Sometimes the "slums" were inherently such desirable areas with such attractive community life that gentrifiers in possession of savings and do-it-yourself resourcefulness achieved renovations that public policy and financial redlining denied them. Frequently they needed to fight interlocked establishments of developers; philanthropists; planners; architects; federal, state, and local bureaucrats; and elected officials to save their spontaneously rejuvenating areas from destruction. Usually they lost these battles.

In the 1960s and early 1970s, young families got into the housing market. But the post–Vietnam War inflation again pushed house prices and interest rates far beyond reach of the poor.

The third approach, promotion of home ownership by long-term, low-interest mortgages, was the only public policy that significantly added to the supply of dwellings. But again, the increased supply was not available to the working poor or to the disabled and others on welfare. Standards and regulations accompanying the government-guaranteed mortgages, reinforced by local zoning codes, mandated suburban sprawl. Sprawl and its consequences are expensive. It is no wonder, given this history, that homelessness has increased in North America and so has the number of families who cannot afford to feed and clothe themselves after they pay half or more of their income for rent in the struggle to avoid homelessness. How could the consequences of half a century of destructive housing policies be beneficial?

One more piece of this puzzle demands attention, because it may hold the clue to a remedy. Almost invariably, in the United States and Canada, the land converted to suburban sprawl was farmland, traditionally owned and worked as family-sized farms. Many farm families were not able to make a reasonable living from their farms, especially when they reckoned their own unremitting, hard labor as a cost. Capital costs for machines and other operating needs kept them always in debt or in danger of defaulting on interest payments. Commodity prices for wheat and other cash crops in years of abundance were sometimes so low that harvests hardly met the costs of their production. High capital costs and low commodity prices were both owing to the fact that tractors, electricity, irrigation piping, and other technology had transformed agriculture. As farmers reached retirement age, it often happened that none of their children, or other heirs, wished to take on the burdens of farming. They were aware of other possible lives, less filled with anxiety and drudgery.

A way out was to sell the farm—better that than to see it foreclosed. Selling could bring in money to pay off debts, and even afford a retirement nest egg; part of the sale price could go into household labor saving devices, releasing farm women to take wage-earning jobs or go into small business for themselves. Most important, selling the land could supply a stake for children and grandchildren to learn skilled trades or professions. Two, sometimes three, generations of a farm family, along with their land, entered the postagrarian economy together.

If the farm was distant from suburb-forming large cities, its purchasers were apt to be proprietors of huge factory farms, executives and absentee owners who did not farm personally except possibly as a hobby and were seeking to increase their acreage. But if the farm was at a fringe of a large city, the best offer was apt to be from developers of suburban sprawl. Sprawl, by definition, is not an intensive use of land, but it is more intensive than agriculture, which is why land prices were high enough for farm families to sell their land willingly, even eagerly, to developers who planned to take it out of farming. Developers and farmers were mutually solving their problems in win-win transactions. Agricultural or park greenbelts that had been designated to encircle cities and constrict their geographical growth, and land zoned for agriculture, melted away under the pressure. Only outright purchases of former agricultural land by public bodies, or gifts to conservation organizations, were able to preserve fragments of former rural landscapes in suburban sprawl. For a society to be able to withdraw so much land from agriculture was an unprecedented economic luxury, but the same changes that were enabling 3 to 4 percent of a population to produce food for the other 96 percent were making withdrawals of small farms for other uses economically feasible. Wasteful use of land became feasible because the land was put to different but more intensive use than formerly.

Sprawl can become less wasteful only by being used still more intensively. If that happens, suburban sprawl will turn out to have been an interim stage, a transition between land in agricultural use and land densely enough occupied to support mass transit, to form functional and inclusive communities, to reduce car dependency, and to alleviate shortages of affordable housing. What kind of pressure can make it not only *feasible* but *necessary* for present owners of sprawl to intensify use of the land, like the farmers before them? A force answering to that description need not be contrived artificially. If it were, it probably wouldn't work any better than the policies of rent control, redlining, and clearances, the contrived social engineering that yielded homelessness and helped erase communities.

In 2011, the first of the postwar baby boomers will turn sixty-five, and many of those not already laid off by downsizing or bankrupt corporations or by cheeseparing "reinvented" governments will choose to retire. In 2015, those born in 1950, the crest of the baby boom, will become a flood of aspirants to retirement, with significant numbers still to come in the next six years. Many, perhaps most, are counting on their largest significant assets, their houses and lots, for retirement nest eggs, or perhaps to provide educational funds—or, more realistically, *credentialing* funds—for grandchildren.

Perhaps money will keep growing on houses, indefinitely. That will take some contriving. In March 2003, a former Federal Reserve governor, Lyle Gramley, was quoted by *The New York Times* as saying that Alan Greenspan, chairman of the Federal Reserve Board, had means for pushing thirty-year mortgage rates as low as 2.5 percent and keeping them there, and the *Times* pointed out, accurately, that this policy would continue to stoke "a storm of home buying and refinancing, promoting consumers to convert the rising equity in value of their homes to cash. . . . But this easy money has done nothing to rejuvenate business spending, and a growing number of economists suspect that war jitters are not the only reason."

In other words, the house price bubble can possibly be deliberately maintained for years to come. But even as Gramley was being quoted, in both the United States and Canada vacancy rates were rising in condominiums, and apartment and house prices and rents were falling in London—not enough to solve the shortage of affordable housing for the poor, but signaling that supply and demand are slowly converging. In any case, sooner or later the bubble must burst, as inevitably all speculative bubbles do when their surfaces are not supported by commensurate increases in economic production. When the housing bubble bursts, whether before or during the coming demographic bulge in retirements, the force driving densification of suburbs could become irresistible in some places, overriding zoning and other regulations as owners of suburban houses and land discover that these can no longer supply cash passively but must somehow earn it instead.

Most owners of suburban lots who feel that pressure will no doubt sell their land and buildings to developers who plan to put them to more intensive use by building apartment houses, low-cost condominiums, and spaces for small businesses—or for whatever other markets promise to be most remunerative. But some resourceful owners will convert their rec rooms to low-cost rental suites, and others may notice that their lots can accommodate one or two small buildings at their rear, which they can either rent or move into themselves, reducing their chores and other upkeep. This will free up their former home and its garages for another family, a bed-and-breakfast, a hair salon, a funeral home, or offices for voluntary institutions or for some of the lawyers who will be needed to handle all the new contracts people are signing. Any number of other possibilities can be visualized: studios, child care centers. . . . If less adventurous owners see that such experiments are producing incomes, they will imitate them.

From the viewpoint of society, it will be preferable for owners themselves to put their lots to more intensive use because their ingenuities will not necessarily require demolition of still serviceable buildings, as developers' ambitions are prone to do, and will almost certainly introduce wider ranges of uses, as well as charm.

Even the roads can respond to densification schemes. Not all roads are community killers like those that have become so common in North America and in countries influenced by North American highway planning. Some roads are famous for fostering community life, as they bring people into casual, pleasant, and frequent face-to-face contact with one another. Many an ordinary Main Street used to do these services, but Main Streets have proved easily transformable into bleak, standardized community killers.

Another kind of road, the boulevard, is capable of serving a district's full ranges of mobility: walks for pedestrians; lanes alongside them for bicyclers and roller skaters; lanes for public transit vehicles, and separate channels for automotive vehicles passing through and those heading for local destinations. Versatile boulevards are little known in North America, and those that do exist are seldom more than ghosts of what they could be. But elsewhere in the world, especially in places with Mediterranean cultures, boulevards are places to which people flock for a stroll when their day's work is done, to see the neighbors, get word of strangers, pick up other news, and enjoy a coffee or a beer and a chat while they take in the passing scene, including sidewalk play of children. People in cities and neighborhoods in much of the world understand their boulevards to be at the heart of their communities. A well-designed boulevard is always well provided with trees along its margins and its medians, because a major concern of serious boulevard designers is to create environments welcoming to pedestrians.

Traffic engineers in North America firmly outlaw, as unsafe, boulevard trees and turnoff channels for local-destination vehicles. Traffic carnage is so high and ubiquitous that it is sensible to give urgent priority to safety. But how do experts and teachers and textbooks know that trees and other boulevard features are unsafe? They don't know, say the authors of *The Boulevard Book,* an exhaustive study of boulevards in the United States, France, Spain, Portugal, Italy, India, Vietnam, Australia, and Latin America. The authors studied accidents and reasons for them and identified specific design flaws; they found that boulevards the world over have fine safety records for all the kinds of mobility they serve. Readers of previous chapters in this book will not be surprised at the real shocker: search as they might, the authors found no studies or other evidence to support the recommendations against boulevards by North American traffic engineers or the conclusions and design exercises set forth in textbooks for university students. These were based on wholly unsupported dogma, nothing more.

Often when presenting designs to traffic officials we were told that a particular arrangement would not be safe. If we asked officials how they knew that, they could not tell us. When we started our inquiries, we were advised on many occasions that both traffic and accident data were available for particular streets . . . but, sadly, the safety information was rarely found. . . . What was the basis of the conclusion that boulevards are unsafe relative to other streets? We have yet to find satisfactory answers to that question.

The authors conclude that the thin air from which the dogma derives in this case is an unexamined belief that boulevards are "heretical" because they embrace complexity and coexistence of multiple movements and users.

An unpopulated boulevard is, of course, just another way to waste money and land and to disappoint expectations, but it may be that when a formerly sprawling suburb becomes dense enough to populate a boulevard with strollers, users of mass transit, and errand goers, it will also have enough clout to lobby for a boulevard, and win it, to replace a stretch of bleak and more dangerous limited-access highway.

Those who love their suburbs as they are, and want to pass them on inviolate to posterity, will not welcome the increased densities and additional uses I have postulated, no matter how enthusiastically they hail "smart growth" in the abstract. Here we must think again of farmers who sold their land. They sometimes sold it regretfully, because they loved their fields, orchards, streams, wetlands, and woodlots. They gave in when these loved assets could no longer sustain them or justify the work of maintaining them. Old suburban residents well enough off to retain their loved houses, garages, driveways, and lawns will be pained at changes wrought by densification, especially if new residents, business proprietors, workers and customers, schoolteachers and children include immigrants from Asia, the Middle East, Africa, South America, and domestic cities, as they most certainly will. Suburban birthrates are typically not high enough for significant densification. A majority of landowners in some suburbs may maintain the status quo. Holdouts will be suburbs frozen in time, to be regarded in future as interesting twentieth-century museum pieces, much as frozen Victorian small towns are interesting nineteenth-century museum pieces. After Victorian architecture fell out of fashion, it was popularly scorned as hideous and for almost a century was treated insensitively at best and ruthlessly at worst, before its appeal was rediscovered. We may expect that frozen suburban sprawls will endure a similar fashion cycle.

Accounts of breakdowns are tedious. Seen from a distance—historical, geographic, administrative, or emotional distance—they make succinct stories. But in close-up view, they consist of too many details, none sufficient in itself; the pieces make sense only when considered together.

Whether densification actually can improve suburbs as places in which to live, work, have fun, learn, and raise families will not depend on adherence to abstractions like *densification* and *smart growth,* but rather on tangible, boring details. Wrong details can all too easily create messes ugly to behold and unpleasant to live with. Suburbanites suspicious of change should not be dismissed as selfish proponents of NIMBY ("Not in my back yard"). They have a point worth heeding: things can be made worse, not better. They often have been, under the banners of good intentions. "God is in the details," as Mies van der Rohe famously said. In wretched outcomes, the devil is in the details.

Rules and regulations will be absolutely necessary to overcome suburban sprawl decently—but not the same rules and regulations that created and encouraged sprawl. Here we must finally confront yet another unexamined old set of suppositions and tools. Only after 1916 did zoning take an appreciable hold on North American culture. The three big ideas that shaped zoning were these:

High ground coverages are bad.

High densities (numbers of people or numbers of households per acre) are bad.

The mingling of commercial or other work uses with residences is bad.

All three assumptions are rejections of cities and city life, devised by utopians and reformers who tried to overcome public health problems and "disorder" with these abstract, dysfunctional solutions. To this day, the three assumptions remain the principal tools of planners and zoners. Even those who do not reject cities and their values, or think they don't reject them, continue to use these three tools—ground coverages, densities, and land uses—as frameworks for shaping built environments. The tools are unsuitable except for creating sprawl, even when they are subject to appeals and amended into incoherence, as often happens.

Zoning rules and tools neglect *performances* that outrage people. What are actually needed are prohibitions of destructive performances. To attend hearings on zoning and planning conflicts is to learn that feared changes are not actually about land uses, densities, and ground coverage but rather about dreaded side effects. The fears fall chiefly in the following categories:

1. Noise from mechanical sources
2. Bad smells and other forms of air pollution; also water pollution and toxic pollution of soil
3. Heavy automotive through-traffic and heavy local truck traffic
4. Destruction of parks, loved buildings, views, woodlands, and access to sun and sky
5. Blighting signs and illumination
6. Transgressions against harmonious street scales.

Any enforceable code depends upon specific standards; an effective *performance code* must, too. Obnoxious levels of mechanical or amplified sound can be specified as decibels from a building or its outdoor property. How an enterprise confines sounds within its premises would be no concern of the code.

Odors pose a unique problem for a performance code because the sense of smell is still so little understood that objective measurements of odor intensity, and quality, are nonexistent. However, we are almost all in subjective agreement about what smells bad. Odors emanating from sewage, rotting food, penned herds of animals, slaughterhouses, and chemicals draw vociferous protests. Aromas from bakeries, restaurants, and backyard barbecues seldom do, unless the food is burning. It would be best for a performance code to accept subjective, popular judgments about offensive smells. However, measurements of particulate matter and chemicals in the air can be expressed as standards applying to pollution from smokestacks and incinerators. Measurements also exist for water and land pollution, including ecologically destructive temperatures of water released from processing plants, and toxic pollution from leaking landfills. A chief advantage of performance codes, especially those updated in light of changing technologies, will be the incentive they offer to solve practical problems that traditional zoning tried to "solve" merely by banishing offenders to poor or politically disregarded parts of town or, recently, to politically feeble parts of the globe.

Protestors against blight do not advocate, to my knowledge, bland little standardized signs and dim lighting (although some architects do); neighborhoods do fear, however, the effect of a billboard city in which giant or glaring advertising signs compete with one another. Maximum dimensions of signs and maximum candlepower of outdoor illumination can be specified.

Building heights and—even more important—length of unbroken street frontages of buildings can be specified, with standards varying for streets with varying existing scales of height and frontages. Scale is not merely a matter of esthetics and taste, although how things look is important. Scale connects with many other aspects of performance; these connections are often really at issue in conflicts ostensibly about uses, densities, or ground coverage. For example, height affects the access of streets or neighboring buildings to sun, sky, and views. Big buildings cast big shadows. They also commonly require demolition of historic or other loved buildings. Maximum horizontal street frontage allowable for an enterprise could accommodate a cabinetmaker's or carpenter's shop, but not a large furniture factory with its heavy and noisy truck traffic.

We are left with destructive behavior of individuals, from which residents and property owners want protection. For example, although people seldom object to unamplified voices in conversation, objectors to permits for outdoor cafés or bars cite louts in the early morning hours who shout angrily and who urinate on walkways and private property, and sick naifs who vomit on walks and gardens. While these and other misdemeanors are indeed matters of performance, they are best dealt with by police and bar owners. Trying to control bad behavior or crimes such as drunk driving obliquely by land use rules doesn't work, and banishes much that is constructive. Insofar as land uses are pertinent to misbehavior, too much of the same thing, unalleviated by other uses—whether residences, bars and clubs, schools, or catchall cultural centers—doesn't work constructively. In cities, differing uses in close proximity tame one another. Even concentrated genteel concert and theater centers from which hordes of people emerge simultaneously, all wanting to nab taxis or buy a drink, breed pushiness and other bad manners.

Agreement to meet provisions of a performance code that has been adopted should be a condition of leasing, renting, buying, or building in a densifying suburb. Enforcement should not be ensured by criminal fines but more directly, by civil court orders requiring noncomplying and noncorrecting offenders to halt outlawed performances forthwith or vacate the premises. The reward for complying is freedom to locate in a popular, performance-protected district and the advantage of being protected too. Another advantage is easy convertibility of premises from one use to another, a process that can take years and incur huge legal costs under traditional zoning codes.

The categories of contention that I've listed are not exhaustive, and no code can remain static. Obnoxious performances of which we now have no idea will doubtless appear in future, while others will become obsolete, just as the fly-breeding manure piles of livery stables became obsolete and, incidentally, at one time, were main reasons for forbidding outdoor cafés and restaurants as unsanitary.

The object of a good performance code should be to combine the greatest degree of flexibility and adaptability possible with the most germane and direct protections needed in the close-up view. The training and credentialing of planners and zoners does not equip them for this task, nor does their work experience. Perhaps collaboration with bright and open-minded young lawyers with a yearning for public service can help to break this new ground. Formulating performance codes will take experimenting, creativity, and respectful attention to public fears as well as hopes. The less time lost in starting, the better.

That is the optimistic view. Pessimistically, we must remember that the vicious spiral of interlocked housing shortages for the poor, loss of inclusive communities, and excessive car dependency had its origins in fifteen years of depression and war. Unwinding that vicious spiral requires peace and prosperity: people must be able to afford sprawl-transforming densifications and renovations. Another rerun of depression and war, stagflation and cutbacks could write finis permanently to the chances of North Americans unwinding this vicious spiral.

One advantage possessed by measures to repair sprawl is that sprawl is so clearly wasteful and inefficient. North Americans prize efficiency. The folk heroes of efficiency of scale—Eli

Whitney, Henry Ford, and legions of efficiency experts in their wakes—long ago convinced North American politicians and populations that economies of scale were responsible for America's high standards of living, which is indeed a partial truth. When items being processed are identical to one another, like pantyhose or parts for cotton gins, cars, or other machines whose development and design are already accomplished facts, economies of scale are easily achieved. The more identical items that are processed, the less overhead cost each item bears, and so the less each item costs.

But efficiency is not a key to unwinding the vicious spiral of credentialing, atrophy of the scientific state of mind, and failures of professional self-policing. These are interlocked evidence of cultural failures to teach and to learn.

The close-up clues to wrong turnings in teaching and learning were identified quickly by 1960s students who complained that they were being cheated of their university educations by being treated like raw materials fed into impersonal production lines.

When human beings are nurtured, efficiency and economies of scale don't apply. Helping individuals become acceptable and fulfilled members of a culture takes generous individual attention to each one, usually from numerous people. Many autobiographies and memoirs attest gratefully to just such life-saving and morale-boosting attention.

At some point in their mentoring, accountants, priests, and other learned professionals who achieved the careers of their dreams, but who then failed to meet their ethical and professional responsibilities, were not sufficiently educated to adhere to civilized standards expected by the culture. Like children, professionals need to be taught right and wrong, and why.

Soon after university credentialing took hold, overburdened professors found that many elementary and high school students had been processed, presumably efficiently, in large lots, but processed so inadequately that they needed remedial work in numeracy, reading comprehension, and expository writing before they could be efficiently credentialed in universities. Nurturing and instructing human beings in a complex culture demands redundancy of mentors and examples. Redundancy is expensive but indispensable. Perhaps this is merely to point out that life is expensive. Just to keep itself going, life makes demands on energy, supplied from inside and outside a living being, that are voracious compared with the undemanding thriftiness of death and decay. A culture, just to keep itself going, makes voracious demands on the energies of many people for hands-on mentoring.

When our own society was much poorer than it is today, it nevertheless managed to meet the inherent expenses and inefficiencies associated with its continuation. How did it do this? How do poor but vigorous cultures manage their continuation today? The answer is that all cultures depend heavily, or have depended heavily in the past, on the natural redundancies to be found in their communities: varied individuals who have varied ways of fitting into the culture and contributing to it. Even a poor society can afford redundancy of mentors and examples, because people in their communities fill those roles by the way, while enjoying themselves or earning their livings by other means: storytellers, skilled tradespeople and craftspeople, musicians, bird-watchers and other nature hobbyists, artists, adventurers, feminists, cosmopolitans, poets, volunteers and activists, chess players, domino players, moralists, life-taught and book-taught philosophers—visible in a community, but invisible to the young when community becomes invisible.

In cultures so deteriorated that nurturing and educating

are in short supply, most of the intellectual and other advantages become reserved for an elite. This is what happened in feudal Europe during the Dark Age following Rome's collapse. Redundancy was rationed as an extravagance when there wasn't enough of it to go around. A fortunate few got tutors and cultural mentors. The rest went without. And even the fortunate few, many of them, were round pegs jammed into square holes. Perhaps the greatest folly possible for a culture is to try to pass itself on by using principles of efficiency. When a culture is rich enough and inherently complex enough to afford redundancy of nurturers, but eliminates them as an extravagance or loses their cultural services through heedlessness of what is being lost, the consequence is self-inflicted cultural genocide. Then watch the vicious spirals go into action!

CHAPTER EIGHT

Dark Age Patterns

As *Homo sapiens* spread over the earth from our species' place or places of origin in Africa, hundreds, perhaps thousands, of the unequal conflicts cited by Diamond (p. 11ff.) must have occurred, followed by countless Dark Ages and extinctions suffered by cultural losers. Then, ten or twelve thousand years ago, the human race started to adopt a radically new economy: agriculture and pastoralism. The old hunting and gathering cultures, which also bartered in found objects such as horns, bones, shells, and reeds; obsidian and red ocher; gold, tin, and copper lodged in surface pockets; wild honey, amber, and captured wild animals, were destined for unprecedented crisis. Henceforth, foraging societies were on the defensive against more powerful agrarian cultures. Foragers resisted, especially those based in mountains and inaccessible wilderness. Sometimes they temporarily made accommodations to agrarian cultures, for instance as concubines, slave traders, or warriors in service to farmers, but they could not prevail against the dominant new cultures and their economies.

With the emergence of agriculture, the world was never again as it had previously been. Almost everywhere, the pristine economies and their cultures went down to defeat and memory loss.

During the ten or twelve thousand years since the emergence of agriculture, agrarianism has dominated the world and the goals of states and empires, shaping their politics, military ambitions, institutions, organizational abilities, fears, and beliefs. Societies most successful at feeding their people from arable land, pastures, orchards, and gardens have been cultural winners and empire builders, just as Diamond found in his analyses.

But that is no longer true. Radical change, comparable in its import to the introduction of agriculture, has been accruing. I have alluded to it from time to time in the preceding pages. Now it is the turn of agrarianism to become a cultural loser. Though not everyone is well fed, the need to eat no longer dictates that most people, or even a high proportion in the West, must live on the land or otherwise work directly with plant and animal production. This change has been a long and gradual time in the making, but is now so dominant that it amounts to a qualitative change in every facet of life. Already the world displays a previously unimaginable redundancy of idled breadbaskets. Upstate New York, for example, once the breadbasket of the northeastern U.S. seaboard, lost out to the fields of the midwestern and western prairies, as did the Ottawa Valley and the Maritime Provinces, once the breadbaskets of eastern Canada. Argentina, Uruguay, Ukraine, and Sicily, once great breadbaskets feeding much of the world, became economic problems rather than solutions, as have the prairie provinces of Canada, along with some prairie heartlands of the United States.

Would-be empire builders have been slowest to take in the great change and its importance. The Germans, who initiated the twentieth-century world wars, forthrightly justified the wars as driven by need for *Lebensraum,* room to live. We may speculate that chiefs and elders of hunting societies, ten thousand years ago, were similarly slow to acknowledge that a source of wealth different from foraging and treasure-finding territory had come to dominate the vanishing world they had known so well. No longer is territory a zero-sum possession of states and empires. Separations and other causes of territorial loss can be win-win events instead of reasons for war or precursors to poverty and failure.

Dismayed at the distraught modern world, we may be excused for supposing it to be in unprecedented crisis. Ingenuity, the new wealth that carries cultural dominance, has generated the industrial revolution, the scientific state of mind and its yields, the rise of democracy, the emergence of a middle class. In sum, human knowledge and skills, and opportunities to use them effectively, have created modern, postagrarian societies. These same assets have provided sufficient stability and corrections (so far) for postagrarian life to sustain itself.

Human capital, per se, is of course not new. It is older than agriculture, for its presence can be discerned in preagricultural Cro-Magnon cave art, in burial decorations, and in prehistoric wind and percussion musical instruments. Creativity and ability to accumulate skills and knowledge are inborn capacities of anatomically modern human beings, much as language is an inborn capacity.

Postagrarian states do not increase their wealth by aggrandizing territories and seizing lands and natural resources—as Japan and Germany learned after losing World War II and subsequently prospering by other means. The key to postagrarian wealth is the complicated task of nurturing economic diversity, opportunity, and peace without resort to oppression. Dark Ages and spirals of decline are in prospect for agrarian cultures that can't adapt themselves to generating wealth through human ingenuity, knowledge, and skills.

Karen Armstrong, in her history *Islam,* summarizes the transforming power of postagrarian culture and the social disturbances it creates. Of education, she writes:

> When resources were limited, it was impossible to encourage inventiveness and originality in the way that we [have done,] in the modern West, where we expect to know more than our parents' generation, and suppose that our children will experience still greater advance. No society before [the postagrarian] could afford the constant retraining of personnel and replacement of the infrastructure that innovation on this scale demands. Consequently, in all premodern societies, including that of agrarian Europe, education was designed to put a brake on the ingenuity and curiosity of the individual, which could undermine the stability of a community that had no means of integrating or exploiting fresh insights. . . . [P]upils learned old texts and commentaries by heart, and the teaching consisted of a word-by-word explication of a standard textbook. Public disputations between scholars took for granted that one of the debaters was right and the other wrong. There was no idea . . . of allowing the . . . opposing positions to build a new synthesis.

While Armstrong's comments above are focused on Middle Eastern and Islamic fundamentalist education, she has much to say about the jolts administered by postagrarian cultures in general. Of the great Middle Eastern empires, which were all in decline by the end of the eighteenth century, she remarks that their decay "was not due to the essential incompetence or fatalism of Islam, as Europeans often arrogantly assume. Any agrarian polity had a limited lifespan." Beginning in the sixteenth century:

> Western society was no longer subject to the same constraints as agrarian culture. . . . There were new inventions in medicine, navigation, agriculture and industry. None of these was in itself decisive, but their cumulative effect was radical. By 1600 innovations were occurring on such a scale that progress seemed irreversible: a discovery in one field would lead to fresh insights in another. . . . Where the conservative society created by agrarian culture had not been able to afford such change, people in Europe and America were becoming more confident . . . in the firm expectation of continuing progress and the continuous improvement of trade. By the time the technicalization of society had resulted in the industrial revolution of the nineteenth century, Westerners felt such assurance that they no longer looked back to the past for inspiration, as in the agrarian cultures and religions, but looked forward to the future.

> An increasing number of people were needed to take part in the various scientific and industrial projects at quite humble levels—as printers, clerks, factory workers—and [they] had to receive some kind of education. More people were needed [and were able] to buy the mass produced

goods . . . [and so lived] above subsistence level. As more of the workers became literate, they demanded a greater share in the decisions of government. If a nation wanted to use its human resources to enhance its productivity, it had to bring groups who had hitherto been segregated and marginalized, such as the Jews, into mainstream culture. . . . [T]he ideals of democracy, pluralism, toleration, human rights and secularism were not simply beautiful ideals . . . but were, at least in part, dictated by the needs of the modern state. It was found that . . . to be efficient and productive, a modern nation had to be organized on a secular, democratic basis. But it was also found that if societies did organize . . . according to the new rational and scientific norms, they became indomitable and the conventional agrarian states were no match for them.

Some things remained the same. In postagrarian cultures, as in agrarian cultures, everything connected with everything else. In either case, if any element of the culture strengthened, the entire web tended to strengthen; if any element weakened, others also weakened.

The complex new culture was not as exportable, nor as controllable when it was exported, as European imperialists supposed. As Armstrong says:

Colonization was experienced by the agrarian colonies as invasive, disturbing and alien. Modernization was inevitably superficial, since a process that had taken Europe three centuries had to be achieved at top speed. Where modern ideas had time to filter down gradually to all classes of society in Europe, in the colonies only a small number of people, who were members of the upper classes and—significantly—the military, could receive a Western education. . . . Society was divided . . . and increasingly neither side could understand the other. . . . Those who had been left outside the modernizing process . . . were ruled by secular foreign law codes which they could not understand. . . . Western buildings "modernized" the towns, often leaving the "old city" as a museum piece, a tourist trap and a relic of a superseded age. . . . People felt lost in their own countries. Above all, local people of all classes of society resented the fact that they were no longer in control of their own destiny. . . . [T]hey experienced a sinking loss of identity.

Even Western people found the transition from agrarian to postagrarian cultures painful, and many still do. But at least Westerners modernized at their own pace and according to their own agendas, luxuries denied most colonies of the West. (Hong Kong is a conspicuous exception.) In Europe and America, modernity was accompanied by increasing autonomy and innovation. In colonies of the West it was accompanied by loss of autonomy and by forced imitation of Western practices, facilities, and aims.

The jolts administered to unprepared agrarian entities by Western empires and later by their joint organs such as the World Bank, the World Trade Organization, and the International Monetary Fund, have already brought into being new Dark Ages, especially in such African countries as Rwanda, Liberia, Congo (Zaire), Sierra Leone, and Zimbabwe, as well as in Cambodia (Kampuchéâ), and Burma (Myanmar). The last two were notably stable and prosperous as agrarian cultures and seemed to adapt comparatively smoothly to French and British overlordship, respectively. Then they sank into postcolonial horrors.

The world today is a bewildering mosaic of cultural winners, groups of people sunk into old or recent Dark Ages and downward spirals, groups in the process of climbing out, and remnants of preagrarian cultures, as well as remnants of declined empires. Even within countries, mosaics of modern, ancient, and Dark Age cultures exist.

Pockets of people patronized as quaint, or ridiculed as feckless and stupid, are sometimes (perhaps always) Dark Age populations still handicapped by the consignment of their cultures and identities to limbo. I knew such a group firsthand in the 1930s, in a bypassed pocket of the Appalachian Mountains of North Carolina. They had lost from memory, largely because of slowly accruing irrelevance, many of the skills they had brought with them from Europe and the U.S. eastern seaboard before their immigration into the mountains and isolation there. They were neither feckless nor stupid people, and their quaintness was inconsequential: sunbonnets, homemade witchlike brooms, safety pins called latch pins, Sioux (the name of a neighboring hamlet) ignorantly pronounced "Sigh-ox." With help from outsiders they regained lost skills and with the help of returning emigrants and their earnings, some of them took new interest in the future and its opportunities.

North Lawndale (pp. 83–85) is part of a modern city's mosaic that includes a place and a people who have sunk so deeply into a Dark Age that they have been unable to maintain even rudimentary community life. North Lawndale and the Chicago mosaic are not unique in Western cities. Ours is a tough species, but individuals and groups subjected to large or small Dark Ages seem to need time and help to recover.

Victims of Dark Ages, especially when they are spatially or socially isolated, or their losses are geographically widespread, have often found recovery impossible, even when they have not gone extinct. Many abysses of mass amnesia must thus intervene between us and the cultures of our ancient progenitors. Unresolvable arguments rage nowadays over whether our early human ancestors were sly scavengers of kills by hyenas, or were bold and brave predators themselves: knowledge that slipped into limbo long ago. Other arguments rage over whether women were always denigrated by men as second-class members of the human race: more unrecoverable knowledge. Even cultures that had writing, like the Minoan of Crete and the successor Mycenaean culture, which apparently conquered the Minoan, remain mysterious to us; a pity, because Minoan art depicts gaiety, fashion, ball games, women with an independent air, and a culture of obviously high achievement, all gone except for its still undeciphered writing, its several dozen stamps for printing alphabetic signs or words, and the cheerful, seductive traces of its culture in its art. We do know that the writing of their apparent conquerors was directly ancestral to Greek, and hence indirectly ancestral to our own—an achievement they passed on before they, too, passed into a Dark Age limbo.

Ancient Greeks, like ancient Hebrews and groups with stories of gods as progenitors, retain wisps of ancient myths wafting ghostly regrets about vanished Golden Ages. Many an age that was Golden compared with what came after it, has indeed vanished.

At a given time it is hard to tell whether forces of cultural life or death are in the ascendancy. Is suburban sprawl, with its murders of communities and wastes of land, time, and energy, a sign of decay? Or is rising interest in means of overcoming sprawl a sign of vigor and adaptability in North American culture? Arguably, either could turn out to be true.

Suppose, when the plaster industry and other contemporary interests were destroying the forests and future fertility of the Fertile Crescent some two and a half millennia ago, someone gifted with foresight had been able to offer advice. What would have been a useful caution? I think it would have been, "Let things grow. Don't let goats eat new growth before the land can regenerate."

Suppose, ten thousand years from now, people of the future who contemplate our own times—which they might aptly call the midpoint crisis between their times and the origin of agriculture—ask themselves what, by hindsight, could have forestalled fatal deterioration of the wonderful North American culture. I suspect the advice might be much like that about the goats: "Let things grow. Don't let currently powerful government or commercial enterprises strangle new departures, or alternatively gobble them as soon as they show indications of being economic successes. Stop trying to cram too many eggs into too few baskets under the keeping of too few supermen (who don't actually exist except in our *mythos*)." If people of the distant future care sufficiently and have sufficiently good documentation, they might note that an American president named Theodore Roosevelt, whose portrait likeness they could still see, carved into Mount Rushmore, had staved off destructive corporate cannibalism for about a crucial half century before it was loosed in the 1960s and intensified in the 1980s.

Climbing out of a spiral of decline or an abyss of mass amnesia is so difficult and chancy, and entails so many ordeals and hardships, that a much better strategy is to avoid falling into terminal messes. A culture that does emerge from a Dark Age is not what a previously failed or conquered ancestral culture would find recognizable. That cultures have been drastically formed and deformed by waging war is a commonplace observation. They must also have been drastically influenced and shaped, physically, socially, and psychologically, by undergoing Dark Ages. The Dark Age following the collapse of Western Rome shaped Europe into a feudal society and culture. Many an obscure Dark Age, imposed in historical times by conquest, has shaped many a demoralized aboriginal culture. Dark Ages are at best grim as reshapers of human life, and unpredictable because they are not subject to wish, will, or plan. They carry with them enormous insecurities, not easily shed, which only drugs or insatiable addiction to power seem to assuage.

How can a culture avoid falling into a Dark Age or near Dark Age, when that appears, objectively, to be its destiny?

Japan managed to evade a colonially imposed Dark Age after Commodore Matthew Perry brought his gunboats to Tokyo in 1853, demanding that the country open its doors to trade with the West. Previously, Japan had adopted a fortress mentality, protecting itself from contact with the dangerous outside world and its cultural disruptions. It continued protecting itself even while it was catching up with the West and in the process transforming itself from an agrarian culture to an ingenuity-based, postagrarian society. Throughout the transformation, the society took immense care to cherish and nurture its own familiar cultural characteristics. It restored its figurehead emperor, glorified the ideals of its samurai, maintained its shrines, and above all cultivated its arts and the highly developed esthetic values they embodied. In sum, Japan assimilated Western ways into its own culture, rather than allowing its own culture to become irrelevant while it was emulating the West.

Japan continues deliberately to follow this policy. For example, it vigorously maintains a program of supporting living national treasures: people who are living masters of Japanese arts—calligraphers, potters and glazers, drummers, gardeners, woodcut artists, puppeteers, traditional actors, carpenters, and others. In return for this support, the national treasures continue to practice their arts and pass them on to apprentices so that neither the skills nor the cultural values and identity that they represent will be lost. Japan's assimilation and further development of Western innovations has been unusually smooth, in spite of war waged against Europe: first against Russia in 1904–5, and then against the Allied powers in World War II. Though Japan suffered horribly from near starvation, nuclear bombing, and bombing firestorms, followed by years under foreign military occupation, it took from its foreign contacts, good and bad, what it wanted to assimilate, without losing cultural memory, identity, and competence. Japan is now abreast or ahead of the West in science-based technology, yet habitually downplays its accomplishments, which avoids provoking envy.

Ireland is almost miraculous in not having sunk into a Dark Age. The conquering English, especially during their brutal invasions, massacres, and oppressions under Elizabeth I and Oliver Cromwell, treated the Roman Catholic Irish as an aboriginal people to be cleared from the land for benefit of the conquerors. Famine, Pestilence, War, and Death devastated Ireland for centuries; its population dropped from nine million to two million in the mid-nineteenth century, partly as a result of famine but also because of English seizure of

Irish lands and forced emigration. But during all these ordeals, the Four Horsemen of the Apocalypse were never joined by the fifth demonic horseman, Forgetfulness. The Irish stubbornly remembered who they were and what they valued, and refused to lose their treasured culture. They accomplished this marvel largely through the fragile medium of song. Their songs prevented them and their progeny from forgetting what they had lost. "Every Irish song is a song of protest," a lawyer in western Ireland told me when I asked him the meaning of a plaintive, haunting solo he had sung at a feast. The Irish suffered civil war and utter contempt from the English, who tried to convince them in every way possible that they were innately inferior. The Irish also suffered terrorism throughout the late twentieth century, much of it self-instigated or self-inflicted; but they never gave up on themselves and the culture they valued.

Song is an extremely effective way of passing a culture down through the generations. As we all recognize, memorable songs and poems that we learn when we are young stay with us into old age. The emotional powers of the arts— authentic arts, not official propaganda—are obviously central to every culture. England now has the lowest productivity of any country in the European community, while the Republic of Ireland has surpassed it. So much for English assumptions of Irish (or Italian or French) inferiority.

Rome's arts were minor in comparison with the culture's other achievements, and Romans themselves were conscious that in this respect they were not creators but lived on borrowings from the Greeks. This deficiency was deemed a strength by Virgil and the emperor Augustus. The same passage of the *Aeneid* that exhorted Romans to fulfill their duty of ruling (p. 55) treated the arts and learning as a digression from the "real" business of life:

> Others will breathe life into bronze with more delicate art—I know it well—will carve marble into the visage of life, will plead cases better, will chart the orbits of the stars and foretell their risings. Your task, Roman, . . .

Perhaps the scanting of emotion and heart, as expressed in the arts, was a major impediment to the endurance of Rome's version of classical culture. The lack must have helped precipitate Roman culture into the forgetfulness of the Dark Age as the empire's institutions of government, trade, and militarism broke down.

The United States has often been equated with Rome by historians and social commentators seeking modern lessons from Rome's mistakes. But fortunately the two cultures differ greatly. American culture is saturated with heart and emotion; it revels in the richness of its indigenous arts. In song alone, America has gospel music and blues; songs of labor unions, cowboys, and chain gangs; hits from musicals and films; country music, jazz, ballads, sea chanteys, rock and roll, and rap; patriotic, war, antiwar, and seasonal songs; advertising ditties; nursery rhymes; school, campfire, drinking, homesick, and love songs; lullabies; revival hymns; plus disrespectful parodies of the lot.

If the hazard is rot from within a dominant culture, or its failure to adapt, obviously the pressing immediate task is for the society to be sufficiently self-aware to recognize the threat of accumulating cultural weaknesses and try to correct them, and so stabilize its complex cultural network. Vicious spirals have their opposites: beneficent spirals, processes in which each improvement and strengthening leads to other improvements and strengthenings in the culture, in turn further strengthening the initial improvement. Excellent education strengthens excellent teaching and research by some of those educated, activities that in their turn strengthen communities. Responsive and responsible government encourages the corrective practices exerted by democracy, which in their turn strengthen good government and responsible citizenship. And so it goes. Beneficent spirals, operating by benign feedback, mean that everything needful is not required at once: each individual improvement is beneficial for the whole.

Ironically, societies (including our own) that were great cultural winners in the past are in special peril of failing to adapt successfully in the face of new realities. This is because nothing succeeds like success, and it follows that nothing hangs on past its prime like past success. Formerly vigorous cultures typically fall prey to the arrogant self-deception for which the Greeks had a word, *hubris,* that we still use. Because a culture is all of a piece, tolerance of commercial false accounting for gaining profit has military equivalents in inflated reports of enemy casualties, along with wishful intelligence about disaffection in enemy ranks. These falsities merely feed hubris; the enemy is a "public" that knows quickly whether wartime false accounting and wishful intelligence are empty bragging. The Bay of Pigs fiasco in Cuba and false body counts in the Vietnam War demonstrated an American proclivity for self-deception. Worse, the incentives for deception—success at sycophancy and pursuit of specious careerism—imply civilian cultural expectations that are shameful whether or not they infect military capability.

History has repeatedly demonstrated that empires seldom seem to retain sufficient cultural self-awareness to prevent them from overreaching and overgrasping. They have neglected to recognize that the true power of a successful culture resides in its example. This is a patient and grown-up attitude to take. To take it successfully, a society must be self-aware. Any culture that jettisons the values that have given it competence, adaptability, and identity becomes weak and hollow. A culture can avoid that hazard only by tenaciously retaining the underlying values responsible for the culture's nature and success. That is a framework into which adaptations must be assimilated. In the case of American culture, and other cultures it has profoundly influenced, such as Canada's, I know no better expression of its core values than the words voiced by Lincoln: "that government of the people, by the people, and for the people shall not perish from the earth." The many indispensable minutiae for expressing and safeguarding that core were added into the culture over centuries; as long as they are not lost to practice and memory, the possibility remains that they can be augmented for centuries to come.

NOTES AND COMMENTS

I. THE HAZARD

Stewart Brand, in *The Clock of the Long Now* (New York: Basic Books, 1999), points out the fragility of preserved knowledge, including that on computer disks and tapes, which are increasingly relied on to preserve newspapers, letters, books, and microfilm. Seeking a strategy to preserve information for thousands of years, he argues that this can only be done by teaching information curators to renew the physical carriers of information before their extinction is threatened; in other words, it has to be done by generations of human beings culturally instructed to fulfill this purpose.

Henri Pirenne (1862–1935), with his pathbreaking books on the early economic, political, and social development of the

Notes and comments follow sequenced chapter texts.

cities of medieval western Europe, laid the foundations for modern understanding of cities. He recognized cities as the engines of economic life and explained why they are. In his *Medieval Cities* (Princeton: Princeton University Press, 1925; paperback edition, New York: Doubleday/Anchor, 1956), he correlates the deepening poverty of Europe through the tenth century with atrophy of city trade in the Mediterranean world (owing to Christian prohibitions against trading with infidels), and the revival of western and northern Europe with revival of intercity trade and, indirectly through Venice, trade with the more advanced Middle East and Asia.

An obtuse foreword by Lewis Mumford to a Princeton paperback edition criticizes Pirenne for his emphasis on cities as economic entities. This is of historical interest in showing how far in advance of the conventional thinking of his day Pirenne's work was, and indeed how far in advance it still is from popular and political—and much academic—understanding of cities, trade, and economic development. Foreign-aid donors and recipients of our time would do well to take to heart Pirenne's lessons on the processes of economic revival and development. His is a basic text for understanding how the world's economic networks operate and how they fail.

The *History of French Civilization* by Georges Duby and Robert Mandrou (Paris: Max Leclerc, 1958; English edition, translated by James Blakely Atkinson, New York: Random House, 1964) takes as its point of departure the nadir in Europe's postclassical fortunes. The quotation citing the misery of early-eleventh-century peasantry (a category that included most Europeans of the time) is taken from p. 7. The first 110 pages explain lucidly how the mundane effects of the slow economic revival shaped feudal France and its institutions, and then also began shaping the Old Regime, which was terminated some eight centuries later by the French Revolution. In those pages an alert reader can also find very early intimations of French cultural characteristics that are significant to this day. The remainder of the book is worth pondering, too, especially by those interested in French literature and art and the formation of culture generally.

The estimate of twenty million deaths of North American aboriginals as a consequence of European invasions and conquests is taken from Jared Diamond's *Guns, Germs and Steel: The Fates of Human Societies* (New York, Norton, 1997; paperback, 1999). Diamond estimates that 90 percent of the deaths were from imported diseases, especially smallpox. Measles and whooping cough, which were relatively innocuous to children of European descent, wreaked havoc among aboriginal children well into the twentieth century. Diamond is fascinating on differential group resistances to two great classes of infectious diseases: (a) those endemic in nomadic and other scanty human populations; and (b) those epidemic in dense populations.

I have learned yet again (this has been going on all my life) what folly it is to take anything for granted without examining it skeptically. When I wrote on p. 11 about the Ainu, I shared the assumption of physical anthropologists that because Ainu have light skins and European facial and skull features and patterns of body hair, they were migrants to Japan from Europe. A mistake. There must obviously have been a time when anatomically modern human beings were generalized— that is, still too new as a species to have distinctive family resemblances associated with specific places. The Ainu represent "preracial" human beings. So we are told by Steve Olson, author of *Mapping Human History: Discovering the Past Through Our Genes* (Boston: Houghton Mifflin, 2002).

The *original* aboriginals of Japan are known to paleoanthropologists as Jomonese. They reached what is now Japan more than ten thousand years ago, lacked "Oriental" facial features and body types, and were apparently the first people to invent pottery. Olson says their fossils indicate that they "represented an early migration of people" north from Australia and southeastern Asia, en route from East Africa. The Jomonese live on in modern Japanese people, contributing a major component to the Japanese gene pool. They also appear to have been ancestors of the Ainu. The other major contributors to Japanese heredity were the Yayoi, rice farmers, metalworkers, and weavers who invaded about 300 B.C.E. from China or Korea, having developed what we now think of as Asian features in the meantime. The Yayoi pushed the Ainu north.

Wilfred Thesiger, the author of *The Marsh Arabs* (New York: Penguin Books, 1967), lived as a doctor among these people for eight years. His marvelous description of their extraordinary way of life and their unique part of the world was reissued in 1985 by HarperCollins, in hardcover, with beautiful color photographs.

Photographs by Nik Wheeler taken in 1974 were published in *The New York Times,* January 26, 2003. The *Times* reported that in 1992, the fabulous reed beds were burned, the lagoons were poisoned, and fugitive human beings were rounded up and executed. This was a sequel to a Shiite Muslim rebellion against Saddam Hussein at the end of the First Gulf War. The marshes have not become a battleground (so far) after the Second Gulf War, but by that point the Marsh Arabs had "virtually ceased to exist," the *Times* reported. The northern approach to the southern city of Basra, where British troops battled to secure the city, is a site—now desert—of some of the former wetlands.

Karen Armstrong's *Islam: A Short History* (New York: Modern Library, 2000) combines religious, military, political, economic, and social history with analysis.

The remark by the fifteenth-century Chinese war official about the worthlessness of China's ocean trading appears in Anthony Pagden's *Peoples and Empires: A Short History of European Migration, Exploration, and Conquest, from Greece to the Present* (New York: Modern Library, 2001). Pagden says that "no one really knows" why the Chinese halted ocean voyaging. Important consequences do not necessarily have important causes or widely known motives—especially when decisions are made by small elites who choose to be secretive.

The old Fort Yukon trapper's remarks were an oral communication, which I have quoted from memory.

For a discussion of the part played by feedback in correcting instability and restoring operating equilibrium, see Chapter 5, "Evading Collapse," in my book *The Nature of Economies* (New York and Toronto: Modern Library and Random House of Canada, 2000; paperback editions, Toronto and New York: Vintage Canada and Vintage, 2001).

The bizarre half century of rapidly acclaimed and murdered Roman emperors was brought to an end by Diocletian, a tough old soldier of peasant stock from what is now the Dalmatian coast of Croatia. He held on to his exalted job, and his life, by promising in advance of his acclamation that he would abdicate voluntarily after twenty years. He kept his promise but was unable to use the time to stem Rome's economic and military chaos. Indeed, his extravagant and radical reorganizations and reforms, although well-meant, probably hastened the terminal collapse.

Rome never did clarify for itself how an emperor should be chosen or removed. It was scornful of kings and dynasties, having disposed of royal Etruscan rule early in its history when it was a small, weak city-state. Its emperors, starting with Augustus, clung to fictional republican titles, while also being worshipped as gods. Moses Hadas, a modern American historian of the classical and ancient world, commented dryly that "the anomaly of an autocrat who pretended to be a republican magistrate entailed serious awkwardnesses in determining the succession." Hadas, *A History of Rome from Its Origins to 529 A.D. as Told by the Roman Historians* (New York: Doubleday/Anchor, 1956).

The unlocked security I observed in Japan in 1972 included shops—often with valuable contents—left unlocked while proprietors were absent for lunch or whatever, leaving customers free to browse without attendants; luggage left unattended while owners wandered away; and many valuable items such as cameras, radios, and shopping bags filled with newly purchased clothing left unwatched, along with shoes, outside temples and shrines. I suspect that last custom may have been the genesis of this pervasive sense of security against theft.

2. FAMILIES RIGGED TO FAIL

My discussion of the sharp mismatch in median incomes and median house prices was published in *Saturday Night* (Toronto, May 1984), excerpted from *Cities and the Wealth of Na-*

tions: Principles of Economic Life (New York and Toronto: Random House, 1984). The objection quoted was by Michael A. Walker, director of the Fraser Institute of Vancouver; it was published in *Saturday Night* (August 1984).

"Housing Resales in 2002 Set U.S. Record," *Toronto Star,* Jan. 28, 2003; "Rents Blamed for 4-Year High in Food Bank Use," *Toronto Star,* Dec. 30, 2002; "Home Ownership Rates Soar," *Toronto Star,* Jan. 23, 2003.

Information on the financial situations of food bank users is from surveys conducted by the Daily Bread Food Bank, in Toronto, and the North York Harvest Food Bank, supplemented by statistics from *Made-in-Ontario Housing Crisis* by Michael Shapcott (Ottawa: Canadian Centre for Policy Alternatives, 2001); *The Growing Season* (A Report for the City of Toronto by the Food and Hunger Action Committee; Toronto, 2001); *Toronto CMA Vacancy Rates and Rents* [1995–2001] (Ottawa: Canada Mortgage and Housing Corporation, 2002); *Where's Home? A Picture of Housing in Ontario* (Toronto: Ontario Non-Profit Housing Association, May 1999; updates, Nov. 1999, 2000, 2001); *Taking Responsibility for Homelessness: An Action Plan for Toronto* (The Golden Report for the Mayor's Homeless Action Task Force; Toronto, 2001); *Depressing Wages: Why Welfare Cuts Hurt Both the Welfare and Working Poor* (Ottawa: Canadian Centre for Policy Alternatives, 2001); *Ontario Works: Making Welfare Work* (Toronto: Government of Ontario, 1998); *Report Card on Children,* a report for the City of Toronto on children living in poverty (Toronto, 2003).

There is no end of statistics on the current mismatches between average housing costs and average incomes in various U.S. and Canadian cities. They are universally horrifying.

In 1993 the government of Canada halted its contributions to municipalities for assisted and nonprofit housing. In 1998 the government of Ontario removed limits on rent increases imposed when a dwelling unit is vacated; the result has been increased evictions. Twenty-two percent of food bank users were either evicted or threatened with eviction in 2001, up from 16 percent in 1998, while average rents rose at twice the rate of inflation in the same period. The *Toronto Star* (Nov. 16, 2002) reported that 4,600 people were sleeping in shelters for the homeless; eight hundred of them were children (probably meaning under the age of eighteen).

The Canadian Automobile Association reported in January 2003 that "it cost the average Canadian motorist $9,525" to maintain and operate a car in 2002, an increase of $1,056 over 2001. The estimates were based on driving 18,000 kilometers a year in a Chevrolet Cavalier four-door sedan. Insurance firms attribute rises in insurance premiums to increased payouts for accident claims and thefts. In the United States, where insurance premiums of all kinds have skyrocketed, shocking car owners, critics of the insurance industry maintain that rising premiums are owing less to claims than to insurance companies' poor returns on their investments, especially bonds. *The New York Times* (June 15, 2003) analyzed "impaired investment assets" of twenty major insurance corporations, indicating that reported losses on airline, telecommunications, utility, and energy bonds "may have already led insurers to raise premiums . . . losses not yet taken as charges against earnings may lead to more." Downgrading by credit agencies increases firms' borrowing costs, so "an insurer may then be tempted to raise premiums," creating "a kind of avalanche effect . . . for insurers and ultimately for consumers." The car-dependent poor are, of course, the consumers who suffer most as remote failures in the economy at large buffet and bruise them.

"Sleep plus Speed: A Highway Deathtrap," according to a *New York Times* article in the *International Herald Tribune* (Nov. 28, 2002), reporting on a conference about drowsy drivers held in Washington at the U.S. National Academy of Sciences. The problem has become sufficiently serious for companies to have produced more than a hundred devices, most of them electronic, to wake up sleeping car and truck drivers. None seems to be surefire; devices to catch drivers when their heads nod, for example, fail because drivers unwittingly soon learn to nap without nodding. The most elaborate device described has been developed by IBM. It shoots a jet of cold water at sleepy drivers, rolls down windows, sounds an alarm, switches radio stations, tells jokes, delivers shock announcements, and monitors drivers' replies to questions for speed and clarity of responses. The company hopes to make the device standard equipment in new cars within five years. James Hall, a former member of the U.S. National Transportation Safety Board, says the reasons why drowsy driving is on the rise include long commutes, the need to work several jobs to support families, an aging society, medications, sleep disorders, and jet lag.

Blandishments to gamble by governments that have become addicted to revenue from casinos, slot machines, and video lottery terminals are effective. Statistics Canada reports that the average annual amount spent by Canadian adults on gambling rose from $130 in 1992 to $424 in 2000. The average in

Ontario was $348, where men living alone spent an average of $1,120 on gambling in 2000; women living alone spent $450, but "women have been growing as a percentage of people gambling in the last ten years," said the director of the Ontario government's Responsible Gambling Council. A Statistics Canada analyst says that the figures are probably the tip of the iceberg, because people "tend to underreport how much they spend on gambling." The data were based on about thirty thousand households.

Much has been written about the General Motors campaign that replaced 146 electric-powered mass transit systems with General Motors gasoline-powered buses. I have drawn chiefly on "Revisiting the American Streetcar Scandal" by Al Mankoff, whose account, written during his retirement after a fifty-year career in transportation, seems the most reliable (*New Jersey Transportation Planning Authority, Inc.,* and *in Transition*; www.njtpa.org/public_affairs/readingroom/trolley.htm). For FBI documents recently obtained under the Freedom of Information Act concerning the bribing of public officials by the GM consortium, see www.njtpa.org/public_affairs/ intrans/scandal.htm.

The best-known essay on these events is by Bradford Snell, who in 1974 was a young lawyer for U.S. Senate investigators and subsequently for the antitrust division of the U.S. Department of Justice. Snell gives a broad and basically true account, but he slipped up on some details and these have been seized on by defenders of General Motors to discredit his report. (The Industrial Reorganization Act: Hearings before the Subcommittee on Antitrust and Monopoly of the Committee on the Judiciary, U.S. Senate; Part 3, Ground Transportation Industries, 93rd Cong., 2nd sess., 1974.)

Snell's critics also maintain that the electric trolleys would soon have been replaced by diesel buses in any case, and as early as 1915 were under threat from unauthorized touring cars and small buses called jitneys ("jitney" was slang for five cents), which, with flexible routes, low fares, and supplemental rush-hour service poached streetcar passengers. So they did, but this is evidence less that electric transit was dying than that a niche had opened for small transit vehicles—something between a streetcar and a taxi—with flexible routes. The niche still isn't filled in the United States or Canada, although elsewhere (in the Friesian district of the Netherlands and in much of the Caribbean, for example) jitney-type vehicles fill the niche nicely. Jitneys were systematically put out of business by municipalities, with the cooperation—to their shame—of electric transit systems, to protect their own monopolistic franchises.

The first jitneys in the United States emerged in Los Angeles in 1914. Before licensed jitneys were hounded out of existence, their numbers had exploded in American cities from coast to coast, reaching a peak of about 62,000 in 1915. In New York, small entrepreneurs—frequently, immigrants from the Caribbean—have since made repeated attempts to reintroduce jitney services. These, too, have been hounded but have been hard to squelch decisively, so badly are such services needed. Currently licensed "dollar vans," for which the fare is actually $1.50, are being legally permitted to supply jitney services in some outer areas of the city. They meet passengers at subway stations or terminals. This uncharacteristic government tolerance of jitneys was the result of a strike by privately owned bus lines, with fixed routes, that had served these areas. The strike was caused by reduction in bus income when passengers transferring from subway to bus were no longer required to pay bus fares. The new transfer policy had been occasioned by vociferous public protests against "double fares." The van fares have not aroused similar protest, apparently because the jitney service is so flexible and therefore speedy. As usual, everything that happens connects with much else. (Oral information from a good friend with wide acquaintance among van entrepreneurs.)

Mankoff tells of the part played by E. Jay Quinby, the naval officer in Florida who tried to warn municipalities that they were being swindled, and the attempts to discredit him because he printed his pamphlets on cheap paper and prepared them in a furnace-basement workshop. Quinby was a maverick who had shocked his wealthy parents by taking a blue-collar job operating an intersuburban trolley out of Paterson, New Jersey.

Mankoff took thousands of photographs of streetcars in New York, New Jersey, and Pennsylvania. More than four hundred of these can be seen at www.almankoff.com/.

The advertisements stigmatizing users of public transit as "creeps and weirdos," associated with "wet dog smell," and touting General Motors passenger cars, appeared in the Vancouver weekly paper *Georgia Straight* of March 13–20 and March 27–April 3, 2003.

The number of prison and jail inmates in the United States reached two million in 1999, up from fewer than 500,000 in 1980, according to *The New York Times* (Sept. 29, 2002). This is said to be the highest rate of incarceration in the world, and to cost some $55,000 per inmate per year.

Generating an economic operation worth $110 billion per year is an impressive feat for criminals, misfits, and unfortunates. The costs of running a prison—money spent largely for prison guards and other staff—are valued sources of income in the poor, backwater communities where large new prisons are generally located. Nowadays most U.S. prisons run by private companies have eliminated costly rehabilitation efforts as "useless"—not true, according to recent meta-analyses, depending on the type of crime (Rodger Doyle, "Reducing Crime, Rehabilitation Is Making a Comeback," *Scientific American,* May 2003, p. 33A [the magazine's department called "By the Numbers"]).

Ontario, which has begun privatizing prisons, promised to monitor the companies responsible for them. However, a Utah-based company, Management and Training Corporation Canada, was found to have violated the province's human rights code in a superjail for fourteen months before the violation (prisoners were forced to wear a racial badge) was noticed by the province. According to the *Toronto Star,* which spotted the violation and which has investigated the practices of private jail companies in the United States, privatization has not proved cheaper, safer, or more efficient than government management. In the Ontario superjail referred to, safety concerns were raised after a 50 percent reduction was made in overnight guards, but the concerns were dismissed. A week later, a hundred inmates tried to escape, and since then half the inmates have been kept on a "partial lockdown" regimen. Privately run jails are a mark of American "reinvented government" that has been picked up by neoconservatives in Canada. They are an extreme example of what I analyze as monstrous moral hybrids in my book *Systems of Survival: The Moral Foundations of Commerce and Politics* (New York and Toronto: Random House, 1991; Vintage, 1994).

3. CREDENTIALING VERSUS EDUCATING

The *Washington Post* survey of computer-science student enrollment was published in the *International Herald Tribune* of August 28, 2002.

"College Degree Worth Millions, Survey Finds" was an Associated Press report from Washington, published in the *Toronto Star*, July 18, 2002.

The panelist/essayist commenting on educational funding and the attitude it revealed was Carol Goar, an editorial writer and columnist for the *Toronto Star*.

John Tibbits, the president of Conestoga Community College, is the advocate for the four-year degree quoted in "Elite Level of Colleges Proposed in Ontario," *Toronto Star*, July 22, 2002.

Robert Gordon, the president of Humber College, said, "We're trying to suggest . . . the designation of some institutions should be changed but making it very clear the idea is not to become a lousy university." The article implies that President Tibbits is envious of Guelph, Waterloo, and Wilfred Laurier universities, which are near his college. President Gordon would like to see the province's twenty-two community colleges become eligible (if they meet requirements applying to four-year degrees) to call themselves Institutes of Technology and Applied Learning; others are suspicious of this as a "marketing gimmick." Thyagi DeLanerolle, the executive director of the College Student Alliance, predicted that a change to "elite status" will "definitely compromise access . . . one of the founding principles of community colleges." Tibbets and Gordon replied that the new status "offers another place for college diploma holders to go when universities won't give them credit."

In May 2003, newspaper advertisements for Loyalist College of Applied Arts and Technology in Belleville, Ontario, invited holders of diplomas to "Join the excitement!" as it announced a new four-year bachelor's degree preparing "leaders for the Human Services Professions." It will be interesting to see whether the degree becomes a required credential, and if so, for what.

"Undergrad Tuition Fees up 135% over 11 Years" is from the *Toronto Star* (Aug. 22, 2002); the information came from a Statistics Canada report issued the previous day.

The chief of Bausch & Lomb was Ronald L. Zarella. The man who perpetuated his insecurity was Jack Grubman, a stock analyst who lost his job. His former employer donated $1 million to the exclusive nursery school where Grubman had applied for acceptance of his daughter, causing another uproar.

For an explanation of why sporadic military production or newly introduced heavy military production can produce military booms (as happened in North America, ending the Depression of the 1930s), but why prolonged military production lacks this power, see Chapter 12, "Transactions of Decline," in my book *Cities and the Wealth of Nations* (cited above).

The Virgil quotation with reference to Augustus is in Hadas (cited above).

Rome decisively defeated Carthage and its brilliant general Hannibal at the battle of Zama in 202 B.C.E., after sixteen years of war. By terms of the treaty, Carthage, which was located in what is now Tunisia, was forbidden to wage war without Roman permission. However, Carthage's trade recovered sufficiently to alarm the senator Cato, who concluded his speeches, no matter on what subject, with "Carthage must be destroyed." In 149 B.C.E., Rome laid siege to the city. When the Carthaginians refused to abandon it and instead manned their walls with improvised weapons, the Romans accused them of breaking the treaty! The siege lasted three years. Here is what happened next, as described by the historian Appian (175–100 B.C.E.), a civil servant of Egyptian origin, loyal to the Romans:

> After penetrating into the city, Scipio [the Roman general] turned his attention to . . . three streets between the market and the citadel . . . lined on both sides with six-story houses from which the Romans were pelted. . . . While one battle was in progress on the roofs another was fought against all comers in the narrow street below. . . . Some were killed out of hand, some flung down alive . . . to the pavement, and of these some were caught on upright spears, sabers or swords. . . . [W]hen Scipio reached the citadel the three . . . streets were set afire. [Romans were ordered] to level a path through the debris as the houses burned. . . . The men . . . overthrew the buildings in a mass. Crashes grew louder and along with stones many corpses pitched to the ground . . . some living bodies too, mostly of old men, children and women who had hidden in the inmost crannies of the houses; some were lacerated, some half burned, and all uttered distressing cries. . . . Others, flung down . . . along with timbers, stones and burning brands, were broken and mangled and crushed into unnatural shapes. . . . [Soldiers, assigned] to remove the debris with axes, crowbars and boathooks and smooth a way for the infantry, shoved the dead and those still living into holes in the ground, using their weapons and turning bodies like blocks. Human beings were fill for gullies. . . . Their legs, protruding from the ground, writhed

NOTES AND COMMENTS / 193

for a considerable while. Some fell feet down, and their . . .
faces and skulls were trampled by the galloping horses, not
through the riders' design but because of haste. . . . There
was the tension of battle, the expectation of quick victory,
the excitement of the soldiery, the shouts of the criers and
blasts of the trumpets, the commands of officers . . . all of
which created a kind of madness and an indifference to
what their eyes saw. Six days were spent on this effort. . . .

The city which had flourished for seven hundred
years . . . was now being utterly blotted out. . . . As Scipio
looked on he is said to have wept openly . . . for a long while
he remained sunk in thought. [From Hadas, (cited above)]

The Carthaginians were a Phoenician people, great navi-
gators, explorers, and traders of the ancient classical world.
Phoenicians were the creators of our alphabet, which we
mistakenly call Roman.

I draw on personal memory of Eisenhower's speech on the
Interstate Highway Program.

"Premier Says He Won't Back Kyoto if Economy Jeopardized," *Toronto Star,* September 7, 2002. The *Toronto Star* of
January 21, 2003, reported that the president of General Motors of Canada, Michael Grimaldi, threatened to withdraw
production and sales of his company's sports utility vehicles
and pickup trucks from Canada if the Canadian government
presses proposals for fuel economy. "[I]f you compromise the
functionality, is the product competitive in the market or is it
better not to offer it? . . . We offer a lot of large vehicles as
well as small vehicles."

Grimaldi said the industry has told the government that it can't reach the goal of 25 percent improvement in fuel economy for new cars and trucks by 2010. "It's an admirable goal but . . . with the product portfolio, the technology, the cost and price issues, we don't see a way to get there." General Motors is Canada's biggest auto assembler and retailer and one of the country's largest employers. It exports about 90 percent of its output to the United States, according to Grimaldi.

Margaret Atwood, "A Letter to America," *The Globe and Mail* (Toronto), March 28, 2003.

The idea of the multiversity was popularized in the 1950s by Dr. Clark Kerr, president of the University of California at Berkeley, but by 1964 he was having second thoughts; he complained that professors were shunting aside the interests of the university in favor of too many activities for which they obtained funding elsewhere. People making big changes need to heed feedback—in this case, that students were being neglected in favor of tasks taken on by the multiversity. Dr. Kerr blamed professors and external funding agencies, and let himself off scot-free for changes in institutions of higher learning that he had persuasively advocated before they interfered with his own administrative interests. For a fuller account of Dr. Kerr's remarks and thinking, see pp. 73–74 in the chapter titled "How New Work Begins" in my book *The Economy of Cities* (New York and Toronto: Random House, 1969; Vintage, 1970).

The president of Carleton University in Ottawa has pointed out, in an interview published in the *Toronto Star* (Jan. 23, 2003), that parents shouldn't expect their children will get the same quality of education they or their older children got. Since the 1990's, the ratio of students to faculty has risen from 16 to 1, to 22 to 1. If you ask students what matters most to them, they say contact with faculty. It's easy to say we'll have places for all those students. It's not possible for us to say the education experience they will receive will be the same.

Other cultures have fallen victim in the past to disconnection between credentials and education. American and European scholars who observed the disconnection in nineteenth-century China gave it the name of *mandarinism* and denigrated it as stultifying.

4. SCIENCE ABANDONED

Thomas Kuhn's book is *The Structure of Scientific Revolutions* (Chicago: University of Chicago Press, 1996).

The destructive plans for Washington Square were conceived and promoted by Robert Moses and his favorite engineering firms. The traffic commissioner at the time of the battle over closing of the carriage road through the square was T. T. Wiley. His successor, Henry Barnes, coined the word "gridlock," predicting a day when New York would be totally paralyzed by cars blocking intersections. While this has not literally happened, gridlock is routinely predicted as the approaching logical conclusion to all traffic jams. Barnes won his reputation first by arranging Denver's traffic lights to halt all vehicles simultaneously at intersections, leaving pedestrians free to cross as they wished, until the lights changed. He was obsessed with the menaces of grid intersections.

A year after impatient drivers were tamed by a change in street direction, traffic humps were added to most streets in our Toronto neighborhood. At least in the case of my block, this may have been gilding the lily. It would have been interesting to have neighborhood traffic and speed measurements before the street-direction change, after the change, and after the humps. One traffic-calming technique is not necessary for all.

I distributed numerous photocopies of the complete clipping from *Chemical & Engineering News.* Optimistically, I thought the information would be enlightening, especially to power brokers and planning staff concerned with plans for the Toronto waterfront, but it seemed not to elicit an iota of interest, except from the city's director of planning, Paul Bedford. Mr. Bedford told me that although he recognized that the elevated expressway could come down—with benefit to traffic movement—this would arouse such opposition from traffic experts in his own department that it would not be practical for him to recommend it.

A monograph by Edward R. Tufte, *Visual Explanations: Images and Quantities, Evidence and Narrative* (Cheshire, Conn.: Graphics Press, 1997), describes Dr. Snow's analysis of evidence in the case of the 1854 London cholera epidemic. The title of Dr. Tufte's paper refers to the importance of the graphics that revealed the data Dr. Snow used:

> By creating statistical graphics that revealed the data, Dr. Snow was able to discover the cause of the epidemic and bring it to an end. In contrast, by fooling around with displays that obscured the data, those who decided to launch the Challenger space shuttle got it wrong, terribly wrong.

For both cases, the consequences resulted directly from the *quality* [Tufte's italics] of the methods used in displaying and assessing quantitative evidence.

The point Tufte makes goes deeper than the fact that displays of data reveal a scientist's acuity of thought about his or her data. Graphic treatment can also, in itself, either instruct or befuddle scientists.

Eric Klinenberg's important findings are set forth, with supplementing tables and photographs, in *Heat Wave: A Social Autopsy of Disaster in Chicago* (Chicago: University of Chicago Press, 2002). Included are sad examples of dead-ended attempts in North Lawndale at community betterment, doomed like those referred to on p. 37.

The population of low-density North Lawndale, which left for the suburbs, was predominantly Jewish; it was thinly replaced by African Americans; the population of high-density South Lawndale, which stayed put, was predominantly Hispanic, augmented heavily by more Hispanic immigration. The late Saul Alinsky tried hard to persuade residents and large businesses not to abandon North Lawndale in the 1960s, with little understanding or help from city officials or planning staff and none from Chicago employers (personal communications).

Statistics on mysterious Canadian job creation in 2002, and the mystified comment I have quoted, come from the business and financial pages of the *Toronto Star.*

For a description of why and how city import replacing occurs, and why it is sporadic, see Chapter 5, "Explosive City Growth," in my book *The Economy of Cities* (cited above). For a diagram showing graphically why a given quantity of economic expansion achieved by import replacement exerts a much more powerful force for economic development and expansion than does expansion of exports, see the appendix that follows the text in that book.

For the effect of the process on a city's own region and the differing effects on more distant regions, see Chapters 3 to 10, inclusive, in my book *Cities and the Wealth of Nations* (cited above).

For a discussion of why the process is a basic form of economic self-maintenance, see Chapter 4, "The Nature of Self-Refueling," in my book *The Nature of Economies* (cited above).

The built-in unsuitability of suburban sprawl for efficient transit systems was researched and well analyzed by Francis Bello in *The Exploding Metropolis* (New York: Doubleday, 1958). He concluded that "there seems no way to provide an efficient mass-transit system that can move people from low-density housing." He did not deal with the potential "jitney" option (see note, p. 187.)

My guesses at why city import replacing has diminished almost to the vanishing point in the United States are these: (a) products all over America have become so standardized that there is no longer much grist for the process; and (b) American production is lacking—an even more serious handicap than standardized production. Lack of production is papered over by importations of foreign capital. The U.S. deficit in balance of payments (the difference in value between what it exports and what it imports) currently makes the United States by far the largest debtor country in the world.

These two symptoms—extreme standardization of products and lack of production—which may be related, remind one of similar extreme economic weaknesses evident in Rome before its collapse. Michael Rostovtzeff, in *A History of the Ancient World,* vol. II, *Rome* (New York: Oxford University Press, 1927; paperback edition, retitled *Rome,* New York: Galaxy/Oxford, 1960), points out that during the "terrible crisis" of the latter part of the second century C.E., when the wealth of the empire seemed limitless, "the people were gradually losing their capacity for work and ingenuity in invention. . . . Routine became more and more powerful in the sphere of creative production."

Writing of the standardization throughout the empire of such ordinary items as crockery and lamps, Rostovtzeff comments on the later empire, "Nothing now except articles of luxury, available to few, finds a distant market." As production dwindled and idleness increased, the Roman shortfall was papered over by the tribute that the imperial power wrung from its satellites and possessions.

Rostovtzeff emphasizes the decay of Rome as decay of morale in rulers and ruled, but he confuses causes and effects. While he describes the breakdown of Rome's economy and its institutions, he develops a circular argument, blaming the deteriorating victims of the breakdowns. Rome's multifaceted troubles are so richly documented and so juicy that everyone since Gibbon has become mired in their very intractability. A great story; especially heard from a safe distance.

5. DUMBED-DOWN TAXES

The *Oxford English Dictionary* gives, as the first meaning of *farmer,* "one who undertakes the collection of taxes, revenues, etc." The word comes from medieval French for a fixed fee. It came to mean, in English, an agriculturist, because farmers were subject to paying landlords fixed fees. The charter allowing a city to farm its own taxes meant that the city could appoint its own tax collectors, responsible to the city rather than to the royal treasury, the church, or a regional warlord. Cities with these powers sometimes undertook what became major regional or national improvements. For instance, the merchants of London, financing a campaign against piracy, laid the foundations of the English navy.

Comparing conditions in Toronto's shelters for the homeless with standards applying to refugee camps in poor countries, a former United Nations aid worker, Rick Wallace, one of the authors of a report on shelters for the Toronto Disaster Relief Committee, says, "Some of the conditions in Toronto shelters are worse than in refugee camps in Rwanda, in terms of space, sanitation and preventative health care practices." A coauthor, Dr. Stephen Hwang, a worker for the health research unit at St. Michael's Hospital, pointed out: "Even a nice shelter is not a good situation from a public health perspective . . . but over-crowding and poor ventilation can only make a sub-optimal situation worse."

The committee's inspectors found that in one Toronto shelter the distance between beds (mats on the floor) was fourteen inches, less than specified in rules for camps in Chechnya or Kosovo. They also found a shelter that had two working sinks for one hundred residents. There were infestations of lice and other pests; several shelters had poorly trained or abusive staff; and fights, theft, and other violations were common. Many city shelters are well run, clean, and sufficiently spacious, the report noted, but added that on some nights some of their guests must stay at terrible shelters, where they can contract diseases or pick up vermin and introduce these to the well-run shelters. The worst shelters were not identified in the report because the authors, who included two doctors and two nurses, said overworked shelter staff have no means to improve conditions.

Sixteen million, three hundred thousand tourists visited Toronto in 2001, a decline of two million from 2000. Most of the decline occurred before the September terrorist attacks on the World Trade Center and the Pentagon dampened air travel. Most Toronto visitors are from the rest of Canada or from U.S. states on the Canadian border. The decline continued, reaching disaster conditions (for hotels and other businesses catering to tourists) in April 2003, when the World Health Organization issued a travel advisory warning people not to visit the city because of the SARS epidemic. The advisory was lifted a week later, when it seemed that the number of cases was declining and that the epidemic was under control, although this was followed by a small spurt. SARS was confined to hospitals and hospital workers from the first, not spreading through the general population. The province had previously stripped its health system of what it considered "redundant" nurses, and of the microbiologists who watch for incoming infections and prepare tests for them. Had any emergency arisen—say, an accident with an unusually high injury toll—the stripped-down health system would have been inadequate to cope.

The emergency that happened to hit was SARS, and although the system had been rendered inadequate by provincial cheeseparing, the system managed to cope, as caregivers and other hospital and public health workers put in working days of twelve hours or more, seven days a week, suffering stress, exhaustion, and probably lowered resistance to infection. The spin doctors of the provincial kleptocracy untruthfully implied that the premier and the province's health minister had not been informed how short the hospitals were of nurses, nor warned that it was imprudent to dismiss the province's five leading medical laboratory scientists. To try to redeem themselves, the premier and minister wept crocodile tears over the immense economic losses to Toronto businesses and workers and promised to launch a comparatively huge provincial advertising campaign urging visitors to return to Ontario. As this is written, in the summer of 2003, the tourists are not yet returning, and citizens are worrying about the ability of hospitals and laboratories to cope with the threat of West Nile fever when the mosquito season starts.

For unknown reasons, in the summer of 2003 the prairie province of Saskatchewan was the most afflicted by West Nile fever. Few cases turned up in Ontario, which was the province most afflicted in 2002.

In the past, the number of jobs in the city and the number of passengers using mass transit rose and fell together. However, starting in 2001, the two statistics parted company. Ridership slipped while jobs grew. The Toronto Transit Commission has not been able to identify why. Even the vicious spiral of higher fares and cuts in services, while it may be partly responsible, does not seem to offer a complete explanation ("TTC Looks for Answers to Drop in Rider Levels," *Toronto Star,* June 17, 2002).

The missing puzzle piece may be supplied by a TTC report published earlier in June, which pointed out that a radical change in laying out routes had occurred:

One of the reasons that the original subways were successful . . . was that they were built on an already-existing solid base of high-volume ridership which had been established by . . . streetcar lines. . . . This strategy was abandoned as TTC's Spadina line was built and other lines expanded. What replaced the earlier strategy was an optimistic notion that high-density development and transit passengers would follow.

The report calls for a return to the "subways second strategy." "It's not build a subway and riders will come, but build it when they are already there."

I am gratified to learn that I'm not alone in being suspicious of fixed rail routes that lack prior empirical feedback. Gordon Chong, the chair of GO Transit, a provincial rail commuter line, previous chair of the Greater Toronto Services Board (abolished by the province), and former vice chairman of the TTC, points out that these bodies, as well as Transport Canada and the U.S. General Accounting Office, are all in agreement that experiments with flexible transit service need to precede fixed rail lines. "After all, a world-class city can't have a lowly bus solve its problems," Chong writes sarcastically. "Maybe it's time we stopped building monuments to our egos and come back to earth." He points out the cost and flexibility advantages of electric trolleybuses and routes, especially in low-density areas (Gordon Chong, "It's Not Sexy, but Lowly Bus Is Effective," *Toronto Star*, April 27, 2002).

The grassroots Toronto Arts Council (I am a member of its advisory panel) has increased its budget and its fund-raising efforts to help compensate for loss of grants from the city to artists and art groups.

After-school courses were restored in response to a savvy campaign by elderly citizens, but tuition fees, which had previously been $1.75 per class hour, were raised in 2001 to $3.50 per hour (halved for seniors) and by 2003 were $6.40 per hour (for seniors, $3.20 or $3.75 per hour). Enrollments dropped during this period from 300,000 students per year to 48,000, and schools participating from several hundred to forty. In addition, registration staff was so severely reduced that only two persons were available in 2003 to take 30,000 registrations in two weeks, another discouragement to would-be students.

The then mayor of Calgary, Al Duerr, speaking at a meeting of Canada's big-city mayors (the C5), in May 2001, said:

> Right now we're a city in a province [Alberta] that is enjoying unbelievable prosperity. We're looking at surpluses of $8 [billion] to $10 billion a year in provincial revenues from petroleum. . . . I should be standing here and telling you that we have the world by the tail, but we don't. The bottom line is, Calgary is struggling. Four years ago we didn't have a significant homeless problem. This fall we're opening two . . . homeless shelters that are going to house over 700 people. We have a huge affordable housing problem. We have transportation problems. We also have Calgarians enjoying incredible prosperity who are beginning to wonder what that prosperity is all about. . . . Calgary collects about 8 percent of the taxes that are paid by Calgarians even though the city pays for virtually all of the essential elements that contribute to the quality of life in the city, other than health care and education. . . . [M]ore money and stronger economies is not the solution—that will not address the fundamental imbalance.

Recounting some of the city's history, Duerr said:

We were primarily a one-industry town until 1982 when the bottom fell out of the economy. . . . This was a difficult period . . . but in many ways it provided the opportunity for the rebirth of Calgary. . . . The downturn caused us to not only diversify our economy but also to rethink what it took to make a sustainable city. . . . We have a much stronger downtown, with more residential units. . . . [W]e are discovering all of those dimensions that make a community. We have a long way to go.

Summing up, he said:

In spite of increased responsibilities and diminishing resources, municipal politicians across the country have continued to deliver good local government. We still have great cities. We will not have great cities on an international scale if we don't come to grips with [the imbalance between cities and other levels of government] (*Ideas That Matter,* vol. 2, no. 1 [2001]).

One might suppose that Ottawa, the national capital, would get a better break from federal members of Parliament than other cities. Not so, says Clive Doucet, an Ottawa city councillor. Like Toronto, Ottawa is a ward of the province of Ontario. Doucet writes in *The Globe and Mail* (Feb. 25, 2002):

I'm considered a successful councillor because only one school has been closed in my ward and no community centre has been shut down. I spend my time running from "Save Our School" rallies to "Save Our Community Centre" rallies. But I never thought I'd see a "Save Our Street" rally. What are we supposed to do—start collecting a partnership fund to rebuild the crumbling street, as we've done for the community centres? It's a trap from which there doesn't seem to be any way out except to rail against the "Canada Problem." . . . Ottawa has more homeless people than Vancouver . . . because we haven't added more than a few sticks to our affordable housing stock in decades.

Federal politicians, like Mr. Martin, are out of touch even with the city in which their parliament is situated, much as Ontario politicians are out of touch with their capital city, Toronto.

In the federal budget for 2000, $1.5 billion was committed to help replace aging medical equipment and reduce waiting times for diagnostic tests. The provinces were given the money to spend, and they used it to purchase icemakers, floor scrubbers, lawn mowers, and sewing machines, probably with the aim of reducing labor costs for hiring maintenance workers. The chief executive officer of the Canadian Association of Radiologists discovered where the money went by digging up sales slips and hospital reports. In some cases, provinces announced they were buying diagnostic equipment but never did so. In Ontario, millions of dollars were given to private-sector firms that subsequently closed their clinics. This exposé was released when the federal government announced another health care grant, in 2003, routed through the provinces. The Canadian Health Coalition, a public watchdog, warned that the government was again courting misuse of funds for medical diagnostic equipment. A spokesman for the federal health minister assured the public that new reporting requirements will ensure provinces are more accountable this time. If only. ("Medical Fund Misuse Feared," *Toronto Star,* Feb. 28, 2003.)

The Greater Toronto Area caucus of members of the federal governing party was able to account for barely half the spending claimed by the federal government in the Greater Toronto Area. Alan Tonks, former chair of the Metro government (predecessor of the amalgamated City of Toronto), is the member of the prime minister's task force on the plight of Canadian cities who could not find information on federal spending in Toronto ("Ottawa Can't Account for GTA Spending," *Toronto Star,* Oct. 8, 2002).

Joe Berridge, a Toronto planner, has made a computer search of subjects considered in the federal parliament of Canada during 2001 and the first half of 2002. Foot-and-mouth disease, of which there wasn't a single case in Canada, was mentioned 172 times; homelessness was mentioned just 19 times. Agricultural subsidies came up 162 times, food banks just once. Rural issues, such as farming and forestry, accounted for 85 percent of keywords turned up in the search. Grain transportation was mentioned more than twice as many times as the automobile, science, technology, high-tech, and biotech industries combined. A Toronto member of Parliament represents an average of 35,000 more people than a rural member, Mr. Berridge pointed out ("Homelessness, Transit Left Off Ottawa Agenda," *Toronto Star,* June 27, 2002).

Richard Gilbert, former director of the Canadian Urban Institute and a former Toronto city councillor, now president of the Canadian Federation of Municipalities, suggests that, while Canada needs local, regional, and national government, it has no need for provincial government. He favors "natural" regions, which in some cases may coincide with provinces, in others not.

He makes a strong case for assigning provincial status and powers to Montreal and Toronto, and explores the pros and cons of the idea gaining acceptance. He thinks a chief advantage to the country as a whole would be a strong urban voice—now lacking—at federal-provincial conferences, the events at which national policies are actually shaped and accepted ("Make Toronto the 11th Province," *The Globe and Mail,* Nov. 26, 1999).

Seymour Freedgood, writing on municipal government in *The Exploding Metropolis* (cited above), noted that the U.S. city is "the child of the State." He said that Chicago's mayor Richard Daley "has summed up the consistent lament of most big-city mayors":

> "I think there's too much local money going to the state capitals and Washington. It's ridiculous for us to be sending them money and asking for it back. I don't think the cities should have to go hat in hand when they need the money for improvements. We're going to have to clarify the role of the locality in relation to state and national governments. The cities and metropolitan areas are the important areas of the country today, but they're still on the low part of the totem pole."

That was in 1958, and that Mayor Daley was the father of Chicago's current Mayor Richard Daley.

For Mayor Bloomberg's budget battle, see *New York Observer,* April 21, 2003, and *The New York Times,* April 20, 2003.

Two recent books by rueful foreign-aid insiders are W. Easterly, *The Elusive Quest for Growth: Economists' Adventures and Misadventures in the Tropics* (Cambridge, Mass.: MIT Press,

2002), and Joseph E. Stiglitz, *Globalization and Its Discontents* (New York: Norton, 2002).

Update: Although nothing has been done, or even officially acknowledged, about the need to reform the provincial-municipal relationships inherited from a century and a half ago, things are looking up somewhat, thanks to voters. In October 2003 the wretched Ontario provincial government was overwhelmingly defeated and thrown out of office by the electorate. This time it couldn't buy the election with tax-cut promises, although it tried. Its successful opponents did not promise tax cuts and instead emphasized restoring services.

The next month, members of the ruling federal party chose Mr. Martin (see pp. 119–22) as their new leader, making him prime minister of the country. During his campaign for that position, Mr. Martin spoke glowingly and often of the necessity of a new deal for cities. He offered no details, but he did invite several big-city health officials to attend a federal-provincial meeting on health and hospital policy—the first time in Canadian history that urban voices have been heard at a federal-provincial policy conference.

Most important, in November, David Miller won a decisive upset victory to become Toronto's new mayor. He has been an outstandingly courageous and intelligent city councillor and is expected to be a courageous and intelligent mayor. So much damage has been done to the city and the administration he inherits is such a dog's breakfast that he has a daunting job, but he has enthusiastic citizen backing. (Declaration of personal interest: Mayor Miller's transition advisory team has two cochairman, of whom I am one; the other is former Toronto mayor David Crombie; see p. 109.)

6. SELF-POLICING SUBVERTED

For distinctions between commercial and governmental ethics, and reasons for the differences, see my *Systems of Survival: A Dialogue on the Moral Foundations of Commerce and Politics,* (cited above).

An especially horrifying instance of delay in self-policing by the College of Physicians and Surgeons in Toronto entailed complaints of health workers as long ago as 1991 that one Dr. Ronald Wilson and his technician were inserting dirty needles in patients' scalps in their EEG clinic. Not until 1996 did the college begin to investigate the allegations, and by that time some 14,000 patients had been exposed to hepatitis B and up to 1,000 of them had been infected. Wilson continued to practice medicine, and patients continued to be exposed to the potentially fatal liver infection, until November 12, 2002, when he was finally found guilty of professional misconduct and incompetence ("Doctor Stripped of His License," *Toronto Star,* Nov. 13, 2002, and "Faster Action Needed," *Toronto Star,* Nov. 14, 2002).

At the hearing, an employee of the clinic testified that he contacted the health ministry of the province to alert officials to the dangerous conditions in the clinic and was told to inform the College of Physicians and Surgeons because that is the body responsible for investigating doctors. At the college, he was told to call the provincial health ministry ("Warnings Were Given Years Before Outbreak," *Toronto Star,* Sept. 2, 2002).

So many people, especially in important corporate positions, had indulged in stock trading illegalities by 2002 that the U.S. Securities and Exchange Commission was unable to keep pace with new cases of alleged fraud, insider trading, and other ille-galities. The U.S. Congress was implicated by default; although it passed laws requiring rigorous oversight of auditing prac-tices, it failed to appropriate sufficient funds for staff to carry out this work. *The New York Times* (Dec. 1, 2002) reported that many of these shortfalls "are traceable to powerful corporate interests on Wall Street and in the accounting profession that continue both directly and through the help of well-placed al-lies in Congress to exert enormous influences on the rule-making process." The *Times* also cited weak leadership in both the White House and the SEC but reminded readers of simi-lar crises surmounted in the past, particularly the Great De-pression. This time, what seems to be ominously different is the participation of the accounting profession itself in the prolifer-ation of business dishonesty. This is quite as shocking as church cover-ups of clergies' crimes against minors.

Acceptance of the belief by wrongdoers that "everybody does it" has become a great enemy of effective self-policing. But fortunately, in reality, everybody does not do wrong. If everyone did, our civilization would have irretrievably col-lapsed. Underlying the democratic ideal of government by consent of the governed is a consent more profound than ex-ercise of the right to vote and obligation to respect the result; it is the consent of the governed to behave themselves—not so much to honor a social contract with authority nor with abstract society as to honor an understood social contract of fair and just behavior toward one another.

"Corporate corruption cases are probably inevitable during the trough of the economic cycle . . . but this wave is different. Some statistics indicate that these fraud cases were actually on the rise during the boom cycle," *The New York Times* reports. "Many attribute the current changes . . . to demographic and economic forces. . . . While the rate of U.S. violent crimes has been declining or flattening over the last decade, there has been a marked increase in accounting and corporate infractions, federal and state officials say. . . . [W]hite-collar crime seems to be the crime of choice of the baby-boom generation." ("Baby Boomers Gone Bad: Fraud Epidemic as U.S. Ages, White-Collar Crime Surges," a *New York Times* report in the *International Herald Tribune* of June 4, 2002).

How the corruption looked from the inside, to those participating in and benefiting from it, is revealed in a memoir by Barbara Ley Toffler, *Final Accounting: Ambition, Greed, and the Fall of Arthur Andersen* (New York: Broadway Books, 2003). Ms. Toffler became the partner in charge of ethics at the Arthur Andersen consulting group after having taught corporate ethics at Harvard University and consulted as an ethics expert for many years. She relates how she was seduced, in one small step after another, by the Andersen organization. In part, the pay seduced her, but attraction and pressure to conform were at least as powerful: "Everyone followed the rules and the leader. When the rules and leaders stood for decency and integrity, the lock-step culture was the key to competence and respectability. But when the games and the leaders changed direction, the culture of conformity led to disaster." Ms. Toffler retained enough of her instinct for danger to resign after four years with the doomed company, but to her credit she stresses how she was taken in, rather than how she got out: "If I got caught up in much of the [company's] culture, what can you expect from young people entering an organization with no idea whether what is happening is normal or not?"

"Normality," per se, is not an instructive ethical guide. What we can expect from young people, fortunately, is that some of them rebel against dishonesty and injustice—even when ill-chosen mentors tell them these are normal—purely because they don't want corruption to be normal. Ms. Toffler is now an adjunct professor of management at Columbia University's business school.

Growing Up Absurd by Paul Goodman (New York: Random House, 1960), and the iconoclastic books by Michael Moore—such as the recent *Stupid White Men: And Other Sorry Excuses for the State of the Nation* (New York: HarperCollins, 2001)—are apropos reading.

Accounting puzzles: "Shifting Trash Cash Draws Fire/City Wants Disposal Costs in Capital Budget/It's Puzzling and It Requires Some Explaining," *Toronto Star,* Jan. 25, 2003.

Interface, Inc., an Atlanta-based multinational, reclaims its nonbiodegradable carpet backing for recycling. This is accounted for as a leasing and service—rather than a sales—contract. Rahumathulla Marikkar, the proprietor of Toronto-based Interface Canada, is a fertile innovator of environmentally sustainable practices, and a charter member of the Green Electricity Leaders' Coalition of Canada.

Natural Capital: Creating the Next Industrial Revolution, by Paul Hawken, Amory Lovins, and L. Hunter Lovins (Boston: Little, Brown, 1999), addresses environmentally and economically sustainable innovations, Interface's among them, and elucidates the need for improved accounting practices relating to the use of natural resources. The paperback edition (also Little, Brown, 2000) suffered a change in title, to *Natural Capitalism.*

But the book is not about natural capitalism, but rather about extremely sophisticated capitalism; and its core subject is indeed natural *capital*. A member of the book club to which I belong planned to report on the book and buy copies for other members of the club, but he found the paperback edition bewildering, considering what its title had led him to expect, and changed his mind. Too bad, because the book is interesting and useful, with much that clarifies direct and indirect costs, benefits, and possibilities of natural resources as drawn on sustainably.

7. UNWINDING VICIOUS SPIRALS

By the end of the 1990s, gentrification was under way in what had been even the most dilapidated and abused districts of Manhattan. Again, the poor, evicted or priced out by the higher costs of renovating, were victims. Affordable housing could have been added as infill in parking lots and empty lots if government had been on its toes, and if communities had been self-confident and vigorous in making demands, but they almost never were. Gentrification benefited neighborhoods, but so much less than it could have if the displaced people had been recognized as community assets worth retaining. Sometimes when they were gone their loss was mourned by gentrifiers who complained that the community into which they had bought had become less lively and interesting.

For analysis of why slum-clearance projects failed as communities and were often inferior to the "slums" they replaced, see my book *The Death and Life of Great American Cities* (New York: Random House, 1961).

Figures on demolition of U.S. public housing by the mid-1990s and for numbers of replacement units are from *Reclaiming Public Housing: A Half Century of Struggle in Three Public Neighborhoods,* by Lawrence J. Vale (Cambridge, Mass.: Harvard University Press, 2002). Of the three reclamation experiments Vale describes, one was successful. In Toronto, planning is currently well advanced on a number of reclamation efforts that emphasize planning cooperation with current residents, a mixture of new uses, such as businesses and market-value residences, and restoration of subtracted streets to knit the areas physically, as well as economically and socially, back into the surrounding city.

In Ontario the total number of farms declined 11.5 percent between 1996 and 2002. In Canada as a whole, the decline was 10.7 percent. In Peel, where Brampton is located, the decline was 24 percent, and in York, where Vaughan is located, 16 percent. The acreage in farmland declined 2.7 percent in Ontario, 0.8 percent in Canada as a whole, 13 percent in Peel, and 9 percent in York.

Ned Jacobs, who was born in 1950 at the crest of the postwar baby boom, has contributed the argument about retirement and aging of his age group, and the possible opportunities this opens for sprawl densification. He has collaborated with me in writing this chapter.

In a master's thesis called "Retrofitting Suburbs: Case Studies of the Evolution of the Urban Fringe" (Graduate Faculty of the Department of Geography, University of British Columbia, 1997; www.telus.net/urbanlogic/retrofit.htm), Michael Mortensen points out how obsolete have become the assumptions behind single-family zoning prevalent for suburban residential tracts. For example, in Canada, between 1941 and 1991, the proportion of lone-parent families rose from 6.7 percent to 13 percent, and of one-person households from 7.1 percent to 23 percent. The proportion of two-parent nuclear families had dropped from 70 percent to 30.2 percent. In the 1960s, a suburban house cost about 2.6 times the average income of a family with one wage-earning head. In the 1990s, when 70 percent of nuclear families had two working heads, the average house cost more than six times their average joint family income.

Mortensen traces the kinds of adaptations, especially densifications, that were made in Vancouver's ring of inner-city suburbs ("streetcar suburbs") built from 1880 to 1920 and how lessons from that experience were useful in further retrofitting of streetcar suburbs and could be useful in outlying suburbs. To resume adaptations in the downtown peninsula and some inner suburbs, Vancouver modified *prescriptive* zoning that had been mandated in its 1929 city plan by developing new *discretionary* zoning codes. These are now in process of being extended elsewhere in the city. Initial guidelines were developed from attention to successful examples, community meetings where citizens expressed desires and fears, and lessons from Christopher Alexander's instructions on incremental, organic planning (*A Pattern Language: Towns, Building, Construction* [New York: Oxford University Press, 1977]). The intents of infill zoning are set forth as

(a) to encourage retention and renovation of existing buildings, ensuring they maintain an architectural style and form consistent with their original character; (b) [to] ensure that new development is compatible with the traditional character of the surrounding street and area; (c) [to]

ensure neighborliness; (d) [to] maintain high quality design; and (e) [to] maintain a range of choice in housing.

The most common form of residential adaptation had been
conversion of single-family houses into duplexes, triplexes,
and quadriplexes. Almost as common had been infill or "coach
house" development, meaning addition of one or two buildings at the rear of a lot or, on corner properties, along the
side. By these means, dwelling densities have been raised to
twice or more of those in postwar suburbs.

Mortensen explains the educational, financial, bureaucratic,
and political changes that made these outcomes possible and
forecast the denser and more mixed and commercial neighborhood centers for which residents in some suburbs are now
asking.

Discretionary zoning seems ideal, provided that its intents
are practical and supported by a politically engaged citizenry.
But I have serious reservations about it because it could be a
disaster when administered by corrupt municipal government, or if planning is dominated by appeal bodies not responsive to citizens. Planners like discretionary zoning because
of the opportunities it affords them to refine and fine-tune
their visions. In Vancouver residents have raised complaints
about standardized results and have objected that citizens are
brought into the process at too late a stage. These reservations
raise the root question: Who has discretion?

Gramley's expectation that Greenspan can keep money growing on houses (*The New York Times,* March 30, 2003) has been
reinforced by Greenspan himself. On May 21, 2003, "he told a
panel of the Congressional joint economic committee that
'the Fed is ready and able to do whatever is necessary to guard

against the remote possibility that a weak economy will trigger a debilitating bout of falling prices.' Greenspan assured the . . . committee that even with the Fed's key economic policy lever, the federal funds rate, at a 41-year low of 1.25 percent, the central bank has other resources to influence interest rates to jump-start economic growth. . . . He said that in addition to pushing the funds rate, which governs [interest on overnight] loans between banks, closer to zero . . . the Fed simply 'could begin buying longer-term Treasury securities to drive longer-term interest rates lower'" ("Greenspan Promises to Fend Off Deflation," *Toronto Star,* May 22, 2003). Greenspan then invoked the specter of the collapsed real estate bubble in Japan as a type of disaster to be avoided in the United States at all costs, but the report of his remarks failed to point out that the severity of the Japanese bubble's collapse was probably owing to Japanese banks' protracted indulgence of bad business debts based on inflated speculative assets that had lost value.

"As safe as houses? Expect most people's largest asset—their homes—to fall in value," says Pam Woodall (*The Economist,* Jan. forecast issue for 2003). Ms. Woodall is the magazine's economics editor. For a fuller analysis of housing bubbles and signs of their fragility—in Britain, Ireland, Spain, Australia, and the United States—see Ms. Woodall's report "House of Cards" (*The Economist,* May 31, 2003, pp. 3–16).

The Boulevard Book: History, Evolution, Design of Multiway Boulevards, by Allan B. Jacobs, Elizabeth Macdonald, and Yodan Rofe (Cambridge, Mass.: MIT Press, 2002), lives up fully to its title and subtitle. The lead author, Allan B. Jacobs, professor of city and regional planning at the University of California–Berkeley and former director of San Francisco planning, is not a relative of mine but a friend. An architecture and planning critic, Philip Langdon, has called the boulevard the "flagship of urban streets" (*New Urban News,* Sept. 2002). Its great virtue, when properly designed, is that it is an *unlimited*-access street, affording entrance and exit to adjoining grids at every corner instead of at a few choke points. A boulevard would be a stunning and functional replacement for the limited-access expressway at the southern perimeter of Toronto's downtown, for example (see p. 76). The quotation about lack of traffic and safety data is from p. 247 of the book, and is amplified by citations, on p. 248, of the dogmatic texts relied on to teach students and guide public officials.

8. DARK AGE PATTERNS

Karen Armstrong, *Islam* (cited above).

The Essential Agrarian Reader: The Future of Culture, Community and the Land, a collection of essays edited by Norman Wirzba (Lexington, Ky.: University Press of Kentucky, 2003).

This is a lament, but not exactly for the good old days of agrarianism, which the editor knows weren't necessarily all that good—unjust to women, xenophobic, provincial, claustrophobic. It is a lament, rather, for what has replaced agrarian life: insensitivity to the environment and even more ruthless treatment of it; frenetic consumerism; decline of democratic participation and community life, stability, and security. It is also a lament that the possibility of building the good things of life on the base of agrarianism is increasingly unlikely, and a belief that this is tragic because an agrarian vision is essential: "food is the most direct link we have between culture and nature," while "industrialism is the way of the machine, the way of technological invention that premises economic success on the exploitation of habitats and communities." Much that the book tells is insightful, important, and sad in the sense that the crooked timber of humanity warps the splendors our biological and cultural gifts present to us for wise, humane, and ecologically respectful lives. In various contexts, the essayists mourn that we do not face honestly who and what we are (creatures dependent on food and the land), although they themselves are reluctant to face honestly that we ourselves are products of nature and part of nature.

The agrarian vision is a faith that, Wendell Berry writes, may yet lead us into "the grace of the world," where we will find our true freedom and joy. I placed myself imaginatively ten thousand years ago and pretended that what I was reading expressed the revulsion of former foragers toward the bondage of peasant life and the loss of adventure, and forager's conviction that "hunting for food is the most direct link we have between culture and nature," while "the way of planting is the way of the scythe and the hoe, the way of technological invention that premises economic success on the exploitation of habitats and communities." They didn't know where they were headed, nor do we.

To Berry, the "industrial mind" is the implacable enemy from which no good can come: It is inherently violent; it impoverishes one place in order to be extravagant in another. It causes war after war. All of these charges could have been leveled by foragers against agriculturalists, and vice versa. Berry sees agrarianism as rooted in sanctity and mystery, like the existence of the world itself. Most of the essayists value agrarianism as a religion, with religious values, and denigrate industrialization as godless, without values. They reject *logos* and take refuge in *mythos* (see Armstrong, p. 17). So it must have been with prehistoric hunters versus planters, each group with an eternal goddess on its side, Diana versus Ceres.

However, these agrarian essays, Berry's included, do employ *logos* to identify much that our culture neglects or does badly, when it could do much better with what is already at hand. Of the surprisingly few changes suggested, those that seem to me to be both practical and potentially most influential are Brian Donahue's proposal that every sprawling suburb use part of its empty open land for an educational farm; and—for economic salvation of at least some family farms— Fred Kirchenmann's "relationship marketing" and synergistic farms; Gene Logsdon's and Wes Jackson's pasture farming and grass farming; and Susan Witt's community land trusts and local currencies.

The "Censorship Watch" column, *Authors Guild Bulletin* (spring 2003), on loss of vital minutiae, has this to say:

What Are You Reading? Part One. [A] survey of 100 U.S. libraries conducted in February 2002 revealed that 85 had been contacted by FBI agents or police officials requesting information about their patrons. Thanks to the USA Patriot Act passed by Congress [in October 2001] the Justice Department has authority to secretly obtain information about the books you read or purchase from booksellers simply by asserting that the information is relevant to an antiterrorism investigation. Librarians and booksellers are prohibited from alerting patrons about the subpoenas, thereby making any legal recourse impossible. In response, Vermont's Bear Pond Books has erased purchase records for members of its reader's club.

What Are You Reading? Part Two. The Total Information Awareness Program (TIA) is the government's latest proposed strategy in the fight against terrorism. Vice Admiral John Poindexter designed the program, which uses electronic "data mining" to enable the government to gather and analyze personal information about every single person in the United States. The system merges commercial and governmental information, which is then scrutinized by the Defense Department for patterns of terrorist activities. In *The New York Times* William Safire detailed what life would be like if the system were ever employed. "Every purchase you make with a credit card, every magazine subscription you buy and medical prescription you fill, every Web site you visit and email you send or receive, every academic grade you receive, every bank deposit you make, every trip you book and event you attend—all these transactions and communications will go into what the Defense Department describes as a virtual, centralized grand data base . . . the supersnoop's dream."

The American Civil Liberties Union has launched a grassroots campaign in opposition to the program.

ACKNOWLEDGMENTS

I am happily indebted for pieces of information, insights, or other valuable assistance to Toshiko Adilman, Mira Baraket, Spencer Beebe and his staff, Carol Bier, Patricia Broms, James I. Butzner, Dr. Decker Butzner, Dennis Cutajar, Ludwig Dyke, Jon Ellis, Chris Full, Ken Greenberg, Riley Henderson, Jack Henshaw, Burgin Jacobs, Professor Richard C. Keeley, Professor Marvin Lunenfeld, Paul B. Manson, Mayor Hazel McCallion and her planning staff, Michael Mortensen, Dr. Fraser Mustard, Bhanu Negenthiren, Margaret Norman, Mary Rowe, John Sewell, Shane Simpson, Professor James L. Spates, Judith Sternlight, Dominique Troiano, David Walsh, and Margaret Zeidler. I am also indebted to Random House's copy chief, Benjamin Dreyer, and production editor Evan Camfield and their staff of meticulous copy editors, who have rescued me from ambiguities, prolixities, and inconsistencies. I am grateful also for the skill and diligence of Aaron Milrad, my lawyer and literary agent; Mary Ann Code, resourceful researcher and fact checker; and Vincent Pietropaulo, photographer—talented specialists with whom it is a pleasure to work.

Most important, this book has benefited from the dedicated care given it by six exceptionally fine editors. Three of these were professionally responsible for assisting the text and me: David Ebershoff of Modern Library/Random House, Anne Collins of Random House of Canada, and Jason Epstein, indispensable editor of my seven previous books, who did not abandon me in his retirement. Another, Max Allen, who had previously edited a book about my work, is also a professional editor but volunteered his expertise as a friend. The other two, Ned Jacobs and Jim Jacobs, I am proud to say are homegrown. Readers would be as thankful as I am for contributions of each of these six if their brilliant questions and polished suggestions could gleam from the text literally, as they do for me figuratively.

INDEX

CITIES AND THE WEALTH OF NATIONS

Principles of Economic Life

Winner of the *Los Angeles Times Book Review* Award for Nonfiction, *Cities and the Wealth of Nations* is "learned, iconoclastic and exciting . . . . Jacobs's diagnosis of the decay of cities in an increasingly integrated world economy is on the mark" (Richard J. Barnet, front page, *The New York Times Book Review*).

Economics/0-394-72911-0

THE DEATH AND LIFE OF GREAT AMERICAN CITIES

The Death and Life of Great American Cities has, since its publication in 1961, become the standard against which all endeavors in the field are measured. In prose of outstanding immediacy, Jane Jacobs writes about what makes streets safe or unsafe; about what constitutes a neighborhood, and what function it serves within the larger organism of the city; about why some neighborhoods remain impoverished while others regenerate themselves. She writes about the salutary role of funeral parlors and tenement windows, and the dangers of too much development money and too little diversity. Compassionate, bracingly indignant, and keenly detailed, Jane Jacobs's monumental work provides an essential framework for assessing the vitality of all cities.

Sociology/0-679-74195-X

THE ECONOMY OF CITIES

"This book is radiant with ideas about what makes cities rich and poor, how cities grow, and how city growth affects national economies" (*The New Yorker*). "*The Economy of Cities* is an astonishing book. It blows the cobwebs from the mind, and challenges assumptions one hadn't even realized one had made. It should prove of major importance" (Christopher Lehman-Haupt, *The New York Times*).

Economics/Sociology/0-394-70584-X

THE NATURE OF ECONOMIES

Like most of the world's greatest ideas, her premise is astonishingly simple: since human beings "exist wholly within nature as part of natural order in every respect," we should look to the processes of nature for vibrant and flexible models of economic planning. Jacobs culls examples from an impressive array of fields ranging from evolution to ecology, chaos theory to cell biology. And because she writes in the form of a Platonic dialogue, a conversation over coffee among five fictional characters, her resplendently original ideas are accessible and clear. Provocative and wise, radical and humane, this book is yet more proof that Jane Jacobs is a truly visionary thinker.

Business/Economics/0-375-70243-1

SYSTEMS OF SURVIVAL

A Dialogue on the Moral Foundations of
Commerce and Politics

With the same far-ranging intelligence and clarity of observation that she brought to her classic works, Jane Jacobs now addresses the moral values that underpin all of public life. Her form is the Platonic dialogue; her sources range from studies on animal behavior to today's headlines. In *Systems of Survival*, she identifies two distinct moral syndromes—one governing commerce, the other, politics—and explores what happens when the two syndromes collide. She looks at business fraud and criminal enterprise, government's overextended subsidies to agriculture, and transit police who abuse the system they are supposed to enforce. She asks us to consider instances when snobbery is a virtue and industry a vice. Above all, in a work of profound insight and elegance, Jacobs gives us a new way of seeing all our public transactions and encourages us toward the best use of our natural inclinations.

Sociology/Public Policy/0-679-74816-4

VINTAGE BOOKS
Available from your local bookstore, or call toll-free to order:
1-800-793-2665 (credit cards only).

Printed in the United States
by Baker & Taylor Publisher Services